CW00351092

Michael Hogben's

A–Z OF
ANTIQUES AND
AUCTIONS

WHAT TO BUY • WHEN TO BID • HOW TO SELL •
WHICH AUCTIONS TO ATTEND • WHO TO BUY FROM

NH
NEW
HOLLAND

First published in 2006 by
New Holland Publishers (UK) Ltd
London • Cape Town • Sydney • Auckland

www.newhollandpublishers.com

Garfield House, 86–88 Edgware Road, London, W2 2EA,
United Kingdom

80 McKenzie Street, Cape Town 8001, South Africa

14 Aquatic Drive, Frenchs Forest, NSW 2086, Australia

218 Lake Road, Northcote, Auckland, New Zealand

ISBN 1 84537 497 5
ISBN 978 1 84537 497 6

Editorial Director: Jo Hemmings
Senior Editors: Steffanie Brown and James Parry
Design: Alan Marshall
Production: Joan Woodroffe

Reproduction by Pica Digital Pte Ltd, Singapore
Printed and bound in Singapore by Kyodo Printing Co (Pte) Ltd

Picture credits and copyright:
Front cover, clockwise from top left: Duncan Soar; PRW Freeman; PRW Freeman; PRW
Freeman. Back cover: Duncan Soar. Plate section: plate 1 (both): Duncan Soar; plate 2 (top):
Duncan Soar; (bottom): PRW Freeman; plate 3 (both): PRW Freeman; plate 4 (top): Duncan
Soar; (bottom): PRW Freeman; plate 5: (top): Alan Marshall; (bottom): PRW Freeman; plate
6 (both): Duncan Soar; plate 7: Duncan Soar; plate 8 (both): Alan Marshall; plate 9 (top):
David Dickinson; (bottom): Alan Marshall; plate 10 (all): PRW Freeman; plate 11: PRW
Freeman; plate 12 (top): PRW Freeman; (bottom): Clive Dunkley; plate 13 (top): PRW
Freeman; (bottom): Clive Dunkley; plate 14 (all): PRW Freeman; plate 15: PRW Freeman;
plate 16 (both): PRW Freeman; plate 17: PRW Freeman; plate 18 (both): PRW Freeman; plate
19: Duncan Soar; plate 20 (top): PRW Freeman; (bottom): Clive Dunkley; plate 21: PRW
Freeman; plate 22: PRW Freeman; plate 23 (top): Duncan Soar; (bottom): PRW Freeman;
plate 24 (top left): Alan Marshall; (top right): PRW Freeman; (bottom): PRW Freeman; plate
25: PRW Freeman; plate 26: PRW Freeman; plate 27 (top): Duncan Soar; (bottom): PRW
Freeman; plate 28: PRW Freeman; plate 29: Alan Marshall; plate 30: PRW Freeman; plate 31
(both): PRW Freeman; plate 32 (both): Clive Dunkley.

Dedication
To my greatest friend and wife, Lesley

Foreword

Michael Hogben – or 'Hogey', as I like to call him – is one of life's wonderful characters. By both owning and running a successful auction house business for many years, he's acquired a wealth of experience in art, antiques and collectables. Whilst I was presenting BBC's *Bargain Hunt* he was often a guest expert, and from the very first time we met, Hogey and I just hit it off. He's warm and friendly, with a wicked sense of humour, and we've been mates ever since. Like me, he's a bit of a wheeler-dealer and he's got a great eye for a good or quirky lot in a sale. Hogey's *A–Z of Antiques and Auctions* is both informative and fun. Like the man himself, it's got to be a winner!

David Dickinson

CONTENTS

Introduction: How it all started for me

My first venture into the business world was at the tender age of 18. After receiving a small inheritance of £500 in 1972, I made up my mind to go it alone, and I decided, having worked for a year in a clothes shop, that the 'Rag Trade' was the place for me. So I set off to open my first boutique, a shop called Mickey Finn in Folkestone. With the help of my brother, Geoff, I proceeded to open another shop in Dover with more shops following. In 1980, having been through a recession, I decided it was time to move on. I'd already discovered that I had an eye for antiques, and I had some nice little pieces at home, but little did I know this was to become my forte.

My next venture was a wine bar in Dover. At this point, wine bars were pretty much frowned upon in England, a situation I found bizarre, living only a short hop across the Channel from France where one could enjoy a glass of wine or beer at any time of the day. After a long, hard struggle with the planning authorities I got a licence for my business. I decorated the wine bar with old enamel advertising signs that I'd bought at auction and in junk shops for between £10–£30 per sign. It is a huge regret of mine that I did not keep those signs, as each would now be worth ten times as much as I paid for them – but that's antiques for you. After a short spell with the wine bar, I decided it was not really for me.

Having turned 30, I decided it was time to get my teeth into something that I really enjoyed. While I was pondering my future, a man known as a 'knocker' came to my door and asked me if I had anything to sell. I said no, but as I was closing the door, he offered me £50 for a painting he spotted on my wall. I declined his offer, but realized that I really needed to know more about the things I owned. This encounter set me on the path to where I am now.

The next day I went to my local library and researched the work of Ethel Lucy Adams, the artist who had created the painting hanging on my wall. I stayed in the library for six hours, reading and learning more and more about art – it was clear to me that this was a hugely exciting subject. The painting I had by Adams was actually worth about £150 – three times what the knocker had offered me. I decided that I wanted to find out more about how to sell my painting, which took me to my first auction. As I walked in to view this sale, I felt like a kid in a toyshop. All I could see were people checking things out and looking at what was what and who was who – in those days auction houses were jam-packed with all kinds of characters. I found the whole experience so exciting that I could not wait to get back the next day for the actual sale.

I decided not to buy anything at my first auction, instead sitting and observing the way a saleroom worked. The auction started promptly at 10 am, when the first lot went under the hammer, which dropped with a loud bang, jolting everyone in the saleroom into action. I knew as soon as the first lot was sold that this was going to be my vocation. I sat in the saleroom for eight hours, watching every lot go under the hammer and writing down every single price. I rushed home after the auction and got stuck into the only two reference books I owned, comparing every price from that day with the prices in the printed guides. To my surprise, a great deal of the lots had sold for well below the prices quoted in my books.

I then spent the next five years learning as much as possible about auctions and the antiques trade. My life was an endless trawl around art galleries, museums, antiques shops, antiques fairs, auction rooms and libraries. Although at that time I was dealing in art, I learnt so much from people who are now my friends and colleagues in the antiques trade. Everyone I met seemed to have a specialist field and took great pleasure in sharing their knowledge with me. It wasn't until I opened my own saleroom in the mid-1980s that I realized how much more I actually had to learn about the antiques trade. By writing this book I hope to share the knowledge I've acquired and throw a little light into the dark tunnel called the antiques business.

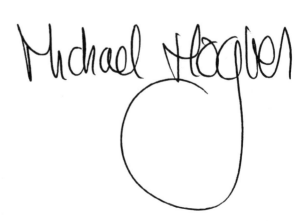

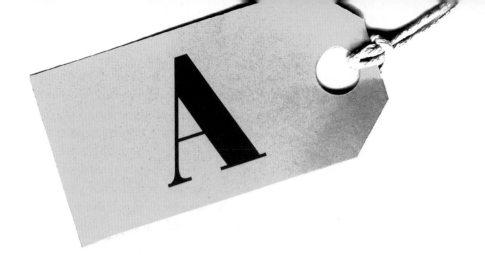

Auctions and Auctioneers

Imagine this scenario. You're on the high street and you're thinking about buying a Victorian chest for £500. It's quite a lot to pay, and you can't afford it, but you love it. What do you do? Well, how would you feel if you had the chance to buy it for £250? Are your ears pricking up?

Then there's that rather handsome 19th-century chest in the upmarket furniture shop close to your home. It's £2,000, but the shop's owner tells you it's a bargain and that it won't be there for long. Would those ears prick any further upward if I told you that you could get the same piece for £800? Then there's the bracelet that would make the perfect gift for your partner, but you haven't got the spare £750 to pay for it. And anyway, I'm sure you'd rather pay £350.

If your ears are now as upright as I suspect they are, then you are ready to take your first steps into the intriguing world of auctions, antiques and collectables. You're ready for the experience that I remember well when I first walked into an auction house. It was a rush of pleasurable sensations, with the added knowledge that there was a possible profit to be made. There were so many interesting characters around me – the auctioneer, the staff and the bidders, and so many fascinating things to look at, touch, discuss and research. And best of all, there were so many bargains to be had! The same surge of excitement I felt the first time I went to an auction still runs through my body every time I make a sale.

Before You Think About Bidding

When you venture into an auction room for the first time, make sure it is a catalogued sale. The catalogue lists every single item up for sale, along with a 'lot number' and a description of each object, which may be very brief or very comprehensive. Most auction houses also give an estimate for each lot, which is basically the auctioneer's opinion of what the item would fetch on the open market. You need to buy the catalogue, as you would be lost at an auction without one, and it is a good investment.

When you visit an auction house, don't be afraid to ask questions, no matter how expensive or rare the items on sale are. The saleroom may look and sound different to your local furniture store, but many of the same rules apply. Like any other shop, an auction house wants to do business – and it wants to do business with you. For example, if you can't find the lot that you're interested in, ask the porter to show you where it is. Why wander around in a daze looking for Lot 135, when you are actually on the wrong floor? And once you've got him or her, ask the porter to pull objects out so that you can look at them properly.

This may seem rather daunting at first, but if you visit a saleroom regularly, you will get to know the staff, and they're usually pretty friendly. You will also notice the same old faces showing up among the bidders, and it's more than likely that some of these are traders. Keep an eye on these 'regulars', and also on the ever-changing lots. In fact, it's a good idea to abstain from bidding on anything the first few times you visit an auction house. Just observe what goes on, concentrating on how the saleroom is run and the behaviour of the people on the floor – you'll be amazed at how much you'll learn as you watch.

The Preview

An auction preview is an enormously important occasion for every prospective buyer, as it is the only opportunity to examine the individual lots, inspect their condition and measure up. So how should you approach viewing day? If you have read the auction catalogue and decided to bid on a few lots in the sale, then you should inspect these first. Never be afraid to ask for help on the preview day; the porters and the auctioneer will be on hand to help you, and to impart their knowledge of each item that will be coming up for sale at the auction.

Viewing Lots

In most salerooms, the furniture is set out in straight lines. This allows easy access to any items that you may want examine in detail. Remember if you are buying furniture to pull the drawers out and check for woodworm. If you cannot get to the item properly, do not hesitate to ask a porter to assist you and pull out the item so you can gain complete access. Once you have thoroughly inspected the item, you can set the price of your maximum bid. (For more on inspecting furniture, see pages 59–60.)

The process of viewing porcelain, silver and jewellery is slightly different than that of viewing furniture. Most auction rooms have a designated porter who will look after you as you view these items. In the case of jewellery, most top salerooms have a special viewing room. Before you are allowed to view the items up for sale, your details will be taken and you will be allocated a number and allowed into the room only under supervision. You can expect to go through a security check when you view any jewellery at an auction.

This system came about as the result of the work of unscrupulous dealers, of whom I have first-hand experience. Many years ago, I placed a very nice one-carat diamond ring with a claw setting in a sale. In the days before the auction, the jewellery was on show for the public to view and handle freely. Two jewellery dealers inspected the ring a couple of days before the auction sale. Little did I know that they had memorized the setting and the size of the diamond. On the day of the sale the prospective buyers came back and asked to view the ring again. As they looked at the ring, they switched it for an inferior one. There was a spate of this sort of behaviour some years ago, which led to auction rooms changing their security systems so that all jewellery is safely stored and shown to prospective buyers under the proper supervision.

Porcelain, china and pottery are usually found in cabinets with the porters handing you one piece at a time to examine. Most auction houses have strong spotlights in their cabinets, which will enable you to check these items for restoration or damage.

Viewing an auction sale properly is as important as bidding on the lot. Time spent at the preview is always time well spent. Don't rush, and make sure you have a checklist for every item you intend to bid on. When you are satisfied with the items you have viewed, you can then set yourself a price limit for bidding at the auction.

Selecting Lots

So, you've perused the catalogue and a couple of items have caught your eye. Say, for example, that one of the objects you favour is Lot 21, a Victorian 'bun' chest with two short and three long drawers. As an auctioneer, I can tell you now that within the brief description 'bun chest with two short and three long drawers' there could be many variables: the quality of the wood, the general construction, the quality of the veneer and the present condition of the chest. Given these variations, you need to make sure that you examine the chest thoroughly. Get the porter to pull it out so that you can look at it from every angle. Open the drawers, take them out and check the joints and look inside the chest. Is there any woodworm? If so, is it treatable? Are you looking for something that you can put straight into your bedroom, or are you prepared to do some restoration work?

At this point a little background research will prove invaluable. Despite years of experience, I still come across objects that I think need further research. Over the many years I have been in the antiques business, reference books have proved to be an enormous help. There are countless books on the subject of antiques, most of which are readily available in libraries and bookshops. These books include lists, price-guides and manuals that cover every area of antiques, including paintings, silver, buttons, dolls, toys, comics – and even more specialist subjects, for example, 1950s china. Using a good reference book, you will be able to check out the history of the bun chest, examine the variations in the object and get a pretty good idea of the value. It's extremely satisfying to discover that your potential purchase is better than you thought. It feels like a lottery win! (For a list of recommended titles to help you with your research, see pages 155–156.)

Putting a Price on a Lot

Perhaps the bun chest you're interested in carries an estimate of £80–£120. You've fallen in love with the piece, it's going to fit beautifully into your bedroom and it goes with other items of furniture in your possession, so now you must decide how much you want to pay for it. Let's imagine that you're prepared to bid up to £140. Don't forget that on top of that figure, you also have to pay a buyer's premium – the auctioneer's charge – of between 10 and 20 percent. This could take your outlay up to £168. You also need to check whether or not VAT will be added to the buyer's premium – if it is, the final figure will be £172.90.

When you've decided how far you're willing to go, jot your top price down in the catalogue and try stick to it. It is possible that when it comes to the crunch, you could get auction fever and decide to pay a little bit more. (To avoid this sort of rash – not to mention costly – behaviour, see pages 132–133.)

Auction Day

If you are anything like me, you'll wake up earlier than normal when auction day arrives. You will feel an excited buzz, similar to what a gambler likely feels when heading out to the races. Will you secure Lot 21 for the price you have set yourself – or will you get it at an even cheaper price? And if the price is pushed above your limit, will you remember how to stave off an attack of 'auction fever'?

Get yourself to the saleroom half an hour before the auction is due to begin. Arriving early will give you time to relax, and will allow you to do one very important thing – go to the main office and register for a bidding number. To get this you'll need to give the auction house your name, address and telephone number.

When you enter the saleroom, you need to find yourself a suitable position. At your first few sales you may not feel confident enough to sit near the front, and may prefer to stand towards the back of the room – a wise move! Once the sale begins, the auctioneer will work steadily; a target of between 100–150 lots per hour is normal in most salerooms. With Lot 21 fast approaching, your heart begins to beat a little faster and your hand begins to twitch in anticipation. You'll find that once you've got your heart set on an auction lot, you'll be able to concentrate on little else – sometimes the excitement is absolutely amazing.

Suddenly, it's time for Lot 21. Your maximum bid is set firmly at £140 – it is there in black-and-white on your catalogue. The auctioneer opens the bidding at £50. The bids continue, rising to £60, £70 and £80, where they seem to stall. The auctioneer says, 'It is with me at £80, looking for £90.' In this situation, don't put your hand up immediately. Pause, take a deep breath and count to three. The auctioneer will not drop that hammer until he is sure there are no further bids, so you can guarantee he will scan the saleroom at least two or three times. The heavy silence in the room is broken only by the ticking of Lot 47, an imposing 18th-century grandfather clock, and the thumping of your heart.

Then someone else bids £90. It goes back to the auctioneer at £100

A IS FOR ADVERTISING SIGNS

From the Victorian age to the mid-20th century there was a huge market for enamel advertising signs. In the days before television and radio, manufacturers still had to attract the attention of the public, so they came up with the idea for these large, metal signs, which were often enamelled and prominently displayed on walls, windows and anywhere else they could be placed. If you look hard enough you will still see some on display today. The signs were usually enamelled in bright colours, bearing a trademark, company name or logo. Today, these signs are hitting dizzy heights at salerooms across England. An early 20th-century enamel advertising sign for BP (British Petroleum), depicting the front of a racing car passing the finishing line and worded 'The Winner', sold for the amazing amount of £28,000 at auction in Canterbury. However, this particular sign was a collector's dream, as it had been kept in storage for over 60 years and was in an immaculate condition. The most valuable signs to look out for are those from the Art Nouveau and Art Deco periods.

Many famous artists worked on these signs, including Harry Rountree (1878–1950). They were created for firms such as Oxo, Players' cigarettes, Singer sewing machines, Fry's chocolate and Cherry Blossom boot polish, to name just a few. Some of these enamel signs are particularly sought after by collectors today, especially early adverts for car manufacturers, such as Lagonda, Bentley, Rolls Royce and Bugatti.

As with all antiques, the condition of an enamel sign is of the utmost importance, so any chips on an item will obviously affect its price. Rust is also a problem, as it cannot really be repaired or restored.

Also, beware of reproductions. These are easy to spot, as they often have a simulated chip mark on the surface and look one-dimensional when compared to the real thing. As with many antiques, my advice is to become familiar with the real thing, because if you do, the fakes and forgeries won't stand a chance. If you do intend to venture into this market, ensure you find out all you can about the item so you can bid with confidence at an auction or buy with confidence from an antiques fair or dealer.

and out to the saleroom again at £110. The auctioneer drops the commission bids (see pages 17, 21–22). At this point, you need to pause and
watch the auctioneer as he scans the room again. Nobody seems to be
bidding, so the auctioneer throws the following question to the floor: 'All
done at £110?'

BANG – at this point your hand needs to go up immediately, clearly
and with courage. The auctioneer will respond: 'With you at £120, Sir
(or Madam).' Then your fellow bidder raises his hand – it's £130 to him.
The bid comes back to you. You raise your hand confidently for £140.
The auctioneer responds with 'Do I have £150 at the front?', but nobody
moves. 'With you at the back at £140.' You hold your breath. 'Are we all
done at £140?' The auctioneer glances at you and drops the hammer. It's
done and Lot 21 is yours. Your first auction has been a success.

A Question of Confidence

From my rostrum in the saleroom I often see individuals blushing as they
bid. I can quite understand this, as you can sometimes feel that the whole
saleroom is looking at you every time you raise your hand. However, rest
assured this isn't the case, as most auction-goers are only interested in a
few specific lots, and more or less switch off during the bids they are not
involved with. Of course, professional traders tend to hover about at
auctions to pick up bargains, and you might find yourself bidding
against them. But don't let this put you off: once you have decided how
much you are going to pay, stick to your guns. If anything, you have the
advantage, because they won't have the same degree of personal interest
and commitment to an object like Lot 21 that you will have.

Yet another fact is worth bearing in mind when bidding against
traders, and it's a scenario that I've witnessed time and time again. Like
anybody else, professional traders will have a a strict budget, and a limit
to how much they will pay for an object. They will fix on a figure from
which they can instantly calculate their potential mark-up and profit. As
a result, a professional trader will tend to drop out of the bidding when
the price reaches a round figure – a point well worth remembering when
you're bidding against them. Imagine the bid is with you at £280 and it
goes to another bidder, who you suspect to be in the trade, at £300. Do
you go to £320? Of course you don't! Not unless the figure is within your
budget – you must always stop at the figure you think the lot is worth.

The best way to feel confident when you bid is to be prepared. By the
time you go to your first auction as a bidder, you will probably have

A IS FOR ARCHITECTURAL ANTIQUES

As more and more Georgian, Victorian, Edwardian and Art Deco houses are converted into apartments, so their original fittings are being discarded, including porcelain toilets, taps, doors, windows, light fittings, switches and wrought-iron gates and fences. These items are worth money to both companies dealing in architectural salvage and collectors. So if you are thinking of restoring an old house, think twice before you discard any items that are original to the building.

I remember visiting one client who was restoring a detached house that dated to the 1950s. The previous owners, who had built the house, had clearly been fairly wealthy, as the fittings were of a superior quality. As I walked into the kitchen my chin hit the ground – it completely epitomized the era in which it was built. Although I could not sell these fabulous kitchen units in the auction room, I suggested that the client contact an architectural salvage company. My client sold the kitchen for £2,000. Each item was gently dismantled and rebuilt in a showroom with a price tag of £10,000.

Old fireplaces and surrounds are always in demand. If you are removing an original fireplace, take a photo of it in situ before you sell, so that a prospective buyer knows exactly what it looks like complete and in position. Many potential buyers will come and dismantle the fireplace themselves. Look out for the early marble fireplaces, as these can be worth thousands of pounds. Tiled fireplaces are also worth selling.

already been to a few sales as an observer, so you'll know the ropes. A popular fantasy about auctions suggests that you can scratch your nose and end up with a £5,000 chest of drawers, or push your hair back from your forehead, only to discover that you have just secured Lot 53, a Victorian chesterfield absolutely riddled with woodworm and in need of extensive restoration. If you prepare yourself by attending a few auctions as a spectator before you become a bidder, you won't be concerned about making this sort of blunder. You will have seen at first hand how auctions work, and you will know how to avoid these sorts of pitfalls.

Paying For Your Winnings

Once you have secured your Victorian bun chest, you will obviously have to pay for it. Most established auction houses will accept credit and debit cards and cheques, as well as cash. Unless you are a regular and are known to the auctioneer, the saleroom will expect you to wait until your cheque is cleared before allowing you to take your item away.

Other Bidding Methods

Say for the sake of argument that the second object that you're interested in buying is Lot 287, a framed and glazed watercolour of a street

A IS FOR AMUSEMENT ARCADES

Although I am not quite an antique myself, I have fond memories of going to the Kent seaside town of Margate with my family in the very early 1960s. Armed with a bag full of old pennies, I enjoyed spending hours playing on old-fashioned slot machines. It wasn't until the 1970s that these older models became outmoded, primarily due to the introduction of electronic versions.

Many were discarded, broken up and dumped, although a few found their way into the hands of collectors. End-of-pier machines like 'What the Butler Saw', 'Test your Strength', fortune-telling devices and even weighing machines that loudly announced your weight to anyone in the vicinity have become very collectable in today's market, along with early pinball machines. Early machines from amusement arcades are a rarity in most salerooms today, and prices can reach anything from £300–£5,000, so they are worth looking out for on your travels. As with any mechanical item, condition is important; if you come across one of these machines that is broken, allow plenty of time and patience to restore it.

Among the items that are very collectable and sought after are the Mills Century one-armed bandits from the 1930s, which have a very obvious Art Deco feel. Similar versions of these machines, dating from the 1960s and 1970s, can be picked up relatively cheaply.

scene, with an estimated price of £30–£50. However, there are more than 200 lots to bid upon before this one comes up. The auctioneer seems to be getting through about 120 lots an hour, which means you have almost two hours to wait. In some instances you might decide to stay and watch the proceedings – a useful practice, as previously mentioned, as it increases your knowledge of the business. However, on this occasion you are too busy and cannot wait around – you need to be somewhere else. So what do you do?

An easy solution is to leave a commission bid. Most auction houses have forms on which you fill in your details and your bidding number, along with the lot number, a brief description of the item and your maximum bid. You decide to set your limit at £60, bearing in mind the estimate is £30–50. However, what happens if there is little interest in Lot 287 – will you end up paying over the odds for a watercolour nobody wants? The simple answer is no. The auctioneer is obliged to obtain this item for you at the lowest possible price. For example, if the bidding in the room stops at £25, the auctioneer will up the bid saying something like, 'It's with me on commission at £30.' This method of bidding is just as effective as being there in person – albeit without the sudden surge of adrenaline. (For more about this type of bid, see pages 21–22.)

A second method of bidding without actually being present in the saleroom is the telephone bid. In this case, you notify the auction house of the usual relevant details, including a telephone number on which the auction house can call you when the lot comes up for bid. Telephone bidding is particularly popular with traders from further afield who perhaps do not want to travel to the auction house if they are only interested in two or three lots. This system isn't used for objects of low value; most auction houses set a minimum price of £100 for telephone bids, and some set the figure as high as £500.

Imagine you've decided to make a telephone bid on a lot in the 'smalls' section (china and collectables). The item is a late-19th-century carriage clock with a repeater action, and it is still in its original leather case. The estimate for the lot is £300–£500. At the initial viewing for this auction, you realized instantly that you really wanted this clock, but before investing in an item like this, you decide to look around and do some research. You visit clock shops and antique shops where you see similar items at prices that range from £700–£1,500. You compare the lot you want to bid for against these items – is it more like a £1,500 clock, or is it nearer in style to a clock priced at £700? Make sure you check the relevant reference books to make comparisons.

Eventually you set a price limit of £550 for your telephone bid. If you include the buyer's premium, the price is actually over £600, but that's what the clock is worth to you. On the day of the auction, a representative of the auction house, often a porter, will telephone you two or three lots before your item comes up. You will be able to hear a certain amount of what's going on in the saleroom. While you are waiting for your lot, it's worth chatting to the person at the other end of the line to get a feel for the atmosphere at the auction, for example, whether or not it is busy. When it comes to your lot, you may have to be a little patient, as most auctioneers use their commission bids, then turn to the saleroom, before checking telephone bids.

The carriage clock opens with a bid at £350, which instantly indicates that there is a strong interest in it. Although you are not at the auction in person, you'll probably find that your heart starts to beat faster as the bidding progresses. The bids come from the room, rising steadily to £370, £390 and £400, before stopping at £420. Now it's time for you to come in and you bid £450. Someone in the room offers £480 and the bidding continues, rising to £520. You make a final bid of £550 – your limit – but someone in the saleroom comes back with £570. It seems the carriage clock won't be yours.

Or will it? There may be some factors that allow you to bend the all-important rule of sticking to your limit and pay an extra £30. At this point, questions will go through your head like lightning – can you afford it? Should you offer more? Will you lose money? You only have a few seconds to make up your mind!

In a situation like this it's worth weighing up your position. This is also a point at which your previous research will prove invaluable. Because you've already done well with the Victorian bun chest and you saved £30 on the watercolour, you can probably allow yourself a little freedom while bidding on the carriage clock. If I were in this position I would ask myself the following questions: how often have I seen a clock like this at auction, and how many did I see while I was researching the item in antique shops? If this is the only one I've seen at a sale, and the few that I had seen in the shops were considerably more expensive, then I would probably up my bid.

Back to the sale, and the lot is with you now at £600. You imagine the auctioneer scanning the room, you and hear the other bidder come back with £650. It's back to you at £700. So, do you up your bid? No, you don't. It's obvious that the person bidding in the room is just as keen as you are, and things could get out of hand. You simply say to the person on the other end of the phone, 'No thank you,' and drop out of the bidding process.

So have you done the right thing? Invariably the answer will be yes. Remember that there's always another carriage clock – and there's always another auction. Think positively: you will find another clock just like it one day. That's one of the greatest charms of antiques and collecting – keeping your eyes open for the piece you lost out on. You never know, you may get the same or a similar clock even cheaper next time, so keep hunting and never give up!

A IS FOR THE
AESTHETIC MOVEMENT

Encapsulating pure style and decadence, the period of the Aesthetic movement was a wonderfully rich time in the arts. As a period it was relatively short-lived – from the 1860s to the 1890s – but it is increasingly an area in which today's collectors are becoming active. Under the motto 'Art for art's sake', the Aesthetic movement thrived on flamboyant decoration, with the work of artist Aubrey Beardsley (who was closely associated with Oscar Wilde) epitomising its spirit and flair.

A particular influence on the movement was Japan. An 1862 exhibition in London showcased Japanese art, and as a result bamboo and ebonised furniture both became very popular. In this respect furniture designed by Christopher Dresser is noteworthy, although now extremely hard to find. Easier to track down are Dresser-designed metalwork, textiles and ceramics.

It is certainly worth looking out for some of the superb furniture produced then. For example, many chiffoniers were of small proportions and so tend to fit in well with the smaller houses of today, and the bamboo pieces also come in many shapes and sizes, from small magazine racks to three-tier étagères. Many such items are decorated in a style called 'japanning', with painted depictions of Japanese villages and people or birds in flight. Overall, this is a very honest period to collect, as items have not been reproduced due to the prohibitive cost of so doing. However, always inspect items carefully, as unsympathetic restorations are commonplace.

Bidding

If you intend to bid at an auction, you will be asked to provide proof of identity, so be prepared to give your name, address and contact telephone number. Some auction houses will also ask for a household bill to further verify your details. Having proof of your identity enables the auction house to know where to reach you if you are successful in your bid but you're not actually bidding in the saleroom. It is very important to remember that if you do make a successful bid, it forms a legally binding contract that you are obliged to honour. Most salerooms also keep a record of registered buyers so they can inform clients of future sales. If you are a specialist collector they will also inform you about items that they feel might be of interest for your collection. Once your details have been recorded and you have been given your buyer's number, you are then entitled to bid in the auction sale.

There are various ways of bidding at an auction sale. Indeed, in my experience as an auctioneer I have seen some very strange methods of bidding. I have had winkers, nodders and finger wavers – you name it, they'll do it! The most common way to bid is to nod your head at the auctioneer or wave your catalogue. People often worry that the auctioneer might miss their bid, but you would be amazed at the sixth sense possessed by most auctioneers. In fact, a good auctioneer can almost feel when someone is going to bid before they actually do.

At one sale at which I was auctioneer, I was approached by a gentleman who informed me that he would be standing at the back of the saleroom. He went on to tell me that if he held his auction catalogue in his left hand it meant he would not be bidding, but if he moved the catalogue to his right hand and placed it on his shoulder, it signified he would be bidding. He also told me that I was not to stop taking his bids until he moved his catalogue again. I still do not know whether he informed me of this so I would concentrate on him throughout the sale, or whether that was the way he actually bid!

Eccentrics like this have been frequent visitors to auction rooms for years. Please don't apply these methods yourself, however – a simple nod or wave of your catalogue will suffice, and will make the auctioneer's job a lot easier.

A useful tip for first-time auction-goers is to stand at the back of the saleroom, so you can see what is going on and who is bidding. If you place yourself at the front of the saleroom, you will find the auction extremely daunting, as you will not be able to bid and turn around at the same time to see who is bidding against you. Everyone likes to know who they are bidding against, whether it is a collector, a dealer or just another novice auction-goer like yourself!

Commission Bidding

As we touched on in the previous section, there is an alternative to attending an auction and bidding on site. If you only want to bid on a couple of lots, or you don't want to stand around all day while you wait for your lot to come up, you can leave a commission bid. A commission bid is a bid that is written on a form supplied by the auction house so that they can execute the bid for you. Before leaving a commission bid, make sure that you attend the sale preview, and ask the auction room for specific information about the condition of any lots you are interested in.

Most auction houses will have a standard form for commission bidding, on which you insert your name and contact details, the details of the lots on which you wish to bid and the maximum bid you would like to leave. Most bidders insert their price, adding '+ one or two bids', in case a similar bid has been left. The auctioneer will be able to advise you as to whether there are any other parties interested in the lot you wish to bid for.

When an auctioneer has been given a commission bid, it does not mean that the bidding will start at the price you noted. Instead, he or she will start at the lowest possible price, and then bid against the room on your behalf. For example, say you have left a commission bid of £300. The auctioneer will be aware of all bids that have been left on that lot in addition to yours. If another bid has been left for £200, and the reserve price is £50, the auctioneer would open the bidding at £50 against the room. Interested bidders in the room will then start bidding against the £50. If the bidding rises to £150 and then stops, the auctioneer would then continue bidding for you, taking the bid to £210, so it is above the other commission bid. You will then have outbid the other interested party and secured the lot. It is not in the auctioneer's interest to run your bid up to the full £300 you have left on commission, as he or she wants you to be able to leave bids in the future with confidence.

It is well known in the antiques trade that specialist collectors prefer to leave their bids with the auctioneer rather than bidding themselves. By doing this, they avoid the danger of rivals competing with them for the sake of it, and the specialist may have spotted something at the sale that a rival has not. I also know many dealers who place all their bids as commissions, as often they will already have viewed the lots, but have another auction to go to on the day of the sale. Dealers' bids are not normally generous, but they do reflect the fact that they are interested in an object – if they can obtain it for a price where they can make a profit.

Those who are new to the business of auctions often wonder why there is so much secrecy about bidding and reserve prices, and why it is not announced at an auction if a lot has been bought on behalf of the owner or sold to a commission bid. Quite simply, all bids and reserve prices are a matter of complete confidence between the client and the auction house. This anonymity is always preserved on behalf of buyer and seller.

Telephone Bidding

Another way of bidding without actually attending an auction is by booking a telephone bid. As previously mentioned, most auction houses will only take this sort of bid on lots that are valued at £100 and over. It is worth noting that, as with other types of bidding, you will need proof of identity – some auction houses will require credit card details to ensure that they are dealing with a genuine bidder.

Bidding by telephone works in a similar way to bidding at the saleroom, but with this method the bidding is done through a representative of the auction house, usually a porter. The auction room will usually phone you a few lots before the item you are interested in comes under the hammer. When your lot comes up, they will keep you apprised of all the action in the auction room. You will be informed of the opening bid,

B IS FOR BANG & OLUFSEN

Bang & Olufsen is one of the most expensive and exclusive pro-ducers of televisions and sound systems. Vintage Bang & Olufsen products, dating from the 1960s, 1970s and 1980s are worth buy-ing, as the quality and design is still superior to many other items available today. Early Bang & Olufsen record decks and speakers are much sought after by collectors, along with television sets from the 1980s and 1990s.

One thing to bear in mind when purchasing Bang & Olufsen products is that most of the items can be integrated, with one remote control for every item you own. Some Bang and Olufsen telephones from the early 1980s were created by Jacob Jensen and many other famous 20th-century designers have developed items for this prestigious company. One current item, the Banana Phone, is sure to be a design icon of the future.

and asked if you would still like to bid. If you wish to do so, your bid will be communicated to the auctioneer. The porter will continue to bid on your behalf until you have either purchased the lot, or reached your price limit, in which case you will drop out of the sale. Telephone bid-ding is a great way to proceed at an auction if you are only interested in a couple of lots, or if you have reason to remain anonymous to the auc-tion crowd. As with commission bidding, many dealers use telephone bidding to avoid a bidding war, and to prevent other dealers from becoming aware of who has purchased the lot.

How Much Should You Bid?

This is a simple question, but it is also somewhat tricky to answer. I can-not state often enough that when you decide to bid at an auction, you should always set yourself a price limit. Whether you are an 'amateur' auction-goer, a trader or a collector, it is crucial that you get the price right. You must think carefully about why you want to purchase a par-ticular lot. There are two words that may help to guide you when bid-ding at an auction: profit and passion.

If you are a trader, or if you are thinking of becoming one, then the only thing to think about when attending an auction is profit. If you buy

B IS FOR BROWN FURNITURE

'Brown furniture' is a term you hear often while walking around sale-rooms and antiques fairs. The term refers to anything that is either solid or veneered dark wood – for example, mahogany – but with none of the heavy carving that the Victorians were renowned for. Although these items were mass-produced, their quality has stood the test of time.

Although woodworking machines were invented early in the 19th century, most furniture was made by small, family-run businesses until about 1870, when mass-production took over. Brown furniture dates from about this time onwards. The companies that produced these goods took up woodworking machines with vigour, using veneering devices, mechanical saws and planing and mortising machines that enabled factories to employ up to 1,000 people. Because production of this furniture was so successful, auction rooms are often filled with mahogany bun chests, dressing tables, wardrobes, cabinets and pot cupboards. This brown furniture has been a staple for auctioneers and dealers alike for many years, although its value fluctuates, and prices have tumbled recently due to the trend for modern and contemporary furniture. However, these low prices mean that brown furniture is one of the better investments in antiques at the moment.

A typical Victorian mahogany-veneered bun chest, mounted on a pine carcass with two short drawers at the top, three long drawers at the bottom and nicely turned 'bun' handles, will currently set you back between £80–£150 at auction. For a piece of furniture that is likely to be over 130 years old, I think this is a bargain.

Other things to look out for are Victorian mahogany wardrobes with triple doors at the front (a piece like this will sometimes be labelled as a wardrobe press). Within the triple doors you will usually find a chest of drawers, hanging space and an area in which store clothes: three pieces of furniture in one. These are currently extremely good value, selling for £250–£400 at auction. Although these items are simple in design and plain to look at, they are of superb quality and craftsmanship, and are extremely useful.

One of the best brown furniture investments is a 'wind-out' dining table, a stunning piece of furniture that was mass-produced in the Victorian period. The action on these dining tables is simple: a mechanism below the table allows you to wind the table in and out with a handle in order to accommodate up to five extra leaves. These tables can extend from about 4 feet, 6 inches to 12 feet, 6 inches in length, seating up to 12 people for a celebratory dinner. When the extra leaves are not needed, they can be stored in a special leaf cabinet, and the table rewound to a cosier length. You can still find these tables for under £1,000 – although I'd advise you to move quickly if you see one, as the price is not likely to stay at this level for long.

One thing to bear in mind when buying plain brown Victorian furniture is that walnut commands a premium. A chest or a wardrobe will be up to £200 more expensive in this wood, while an extendable dining table could be as much as £1,000 more than an example in mahogany. A pair of walnut bedside cabinets might set you back £300–£500; this seems expensive, but I can assure you that they are a good investment. However, before you buy a lot with this description you must check that the cabinets are a matched pair – for example, if you placed them on each side of the bed, would the doors open the correct way, i.e. in opposite directions?

Rosewood is another material which was widely used to make furniture in the Victorian era. It is a very hard wood, and is easy to distinguish from mahogany or oak because it has black lines running through the heavy grain. It is also extremely heavy.

The list of brown furniture items available is enormous, including davenports, card tables, coffee tables and side tables, in addition to the objects discussed above. Because so much brown furniture was produced in the late Victorian period, and because so many items have survived, only an outstanding example will make substantial money at an auction.

a particular lot at £100, will you be able to sell it for more? If the top price you think you can achieve for this object is £150, then anything you pay over £50 for the item is going to cut into your profit quite significantly. Most dealers expect to make at least a 50 percent profit on any item they buy. Personally, I do not begrudge dealers a good profit, as I know how hard they have to work to source the goods they sell. Many dealers travel hundreds of miles to attend sales – and some auction rooms can be pretty bleak in the winter months.

If you are a private buyer or collector, then passion should dictate your bid, which means it all comes down to what you can afford. If you have seen an object in an antique shop or at an antiques fair priced at £300, but you can secure the same item for £200 at an auction, then you have done well. And, of course, you've saved yourself £100. One of the reasons so many private collectors attend auctions is that sourcing items personally, rather than through a third-party, is enormously enjoyable. If you are an avid collector, there is no better buzz than knowing you've bagged a bargain. However, once you're actually in an auction room, you need to keep your wits about you, as bidding can be a minefield. You will undoubtedly face other collectors bidding against you at some point, and dealers will also bid against you, often pushing up the price. This may mean that you'll pay a bit more than you expected for some collectables, but that's where confidence and experience come in.

Completing Your Bid

If you are lucky enough to secure the lot you were after, don't forget that you still have to pay the buyer's premium. This is usually 10–20 percent of the price you bid under the hammer. You will usually also have to add VAT to the cost of your bid. Once you've paid for the lot, which you should do as swiftly as possible, you will be able to collect the item. Most auction houses have storage available, but will charge a daily rate to store your lot.

Building A Collection

If I had a penny for every time someone has asked me how to make money out of antiques I would be a wealthy man. But when I'm asked this question, I always give the same answer – build a collection. This involves becoming a specialist in a particular field. Whether your passion is for Georgian furniture, longcase clocks, Art Deco or Modernist objects, you will need to learn about every aspect of your chosen subject.

For example, I once knew a couple that fell in love with the works of the influential ceramicist Clarice Cliff (1899–1972). Initially, this couple knew little about Cliff or her work, but they made it a mission to understand everything there was to know about her. They started by reading books about Cliff, and then began to visit antiques fairs, shops and auctions. By doing this, they were able to touch and feel Cliff's work, studying the quality, patterns and designs of items for sale. They also learned how to check for signs of restoration, and ensured that any items they bought were the best they could afford. By doing such extensive background work, they came to realize that, although Clarice Cliff was extremely prolific, some of her works were better than others. (Certain examples of Cliff's works will always be more expensive; for example, those with geometric designs.)

As time progressed, the pair built up an extremely impressive collection of objects designed by Clarice Cliff. As an auctioneer, I was lucky to be able to value this collection and was surprised at how little they had managed to pay for some pieces. But more significantly, during the five years that these enthusiasts had been accumulating works by Cliff, the collection had steadily increased in value.

As a result of collecting works by Clarice Cliff, the pair extended their interest to the entire Art Deco period. Their collection built up to include some fine Art Deco furniture, paintings and china – they even ended up buying a house from the period. Then, with the experience they acquired, they took the leap into the antiques world. At first they had a small antiques stall, but within a couple of years they owned a shop that specialized in Clarice Cliff and Art Deco objects.

Becoming a specialist is not an easy option: it takes a lot of dedication and hard work. But from my experience, it is the dealers that specialize in collections who gain the most satisfaction and profit from auctions.

B IS FOR BUCHAN WARE

Buchan is a small Scottish pottery factory that produced some very collectable handmade and hand-painted pots, vases, dishes and everyday items during the 1950s–1970s. The subtle, yet stylized decoration of these pieces often has a green background with brown highlights. Some pieces can still be found for £5–£10.

Commission and Charges

Like any business, an auction house needs to make a profit to survive. The way that they make money is to charge the vendor a commission charge, and also to charge buyers a premium.

Commission charges vary, but some are as high as 25 percent. However, many auction houses also offer negotiable commission deals. For example, an auction house may charge 15 percent commission on items that sell at less than £1,000, but for items that sell for more than £1,000, the commission rate becomes negotiable. If you are selling a number of items at auction, it is always worth negotiating the final commission that you will have to pay. For instance, you may want to sell at auction the entire contents of a house you have inherited. If this is the case, the auctioneers are likely to negotiate a competitive commission rate, which may be as low as 5 percent.

On top of the commission rate and VAT, auction houses usually charge vendors an extra two percent to cover items such as insurance, transport and catalogue costs. In is vital that you realize how much you are going to be charged for these items **before** you put your goods up for auction.

Another charge that vendors need to make themselves aware of is the 'unsold' charge. If an item has been entered into an auction and illustrated in the catalogue, but it has failed to attract a buyer – perhaps because the reserve price was too high, or the sale was quiet – the

TEN IMPORTANT QUESTIONS ALL SELLERS SHOULD ASK THE AUCTIONEER

1) What is your commission rate, and is it negotiable?
2) What are the transport and storage charges?
3) What are the charges for illustrations in the catalogue?
4) What percentage do you charge for insurance, and what cover can I expect?
5) If a lot remains unsold, will I have to pay a fee? If so, how much per lot?
6) If I think your valuation is too low, can I place a higher reserve on the item?
7) Do you produce a glossy catalogue?
8) Where can I expect to see the auction advertised?
9) Does the auction room have a website?
10) When can I expect settlement for any goods sold?

vendor may still be liable for an additional charge. Thus, before you submit any item to an auction house, you must check up on this matter, as unsold fees can be quite pricey.

Finding the Right Auction House

If you decide to sell something at auction, I would recommend that you consult at least two salerooms beforehand to discover who will offer you the best rate of commission. If you have a specialist item – for example, an original piece of Arts and Crafts furniture – you should really take it to an auction room that deals specifically with this type of object, and produces a glossy catalogue with extensive illustrations. Although London is known for its major salerooms, there are plenty of provincial salerooms that offer similar services, often at more competitive rates (see pages 153–154 for details of recommended auction houses). It pays to do your research and listen to what experts tell you, as the cautionary tale that follows shows.

A man once approached me wishing to put a painting up for auction. I gave him an estimate of between £200–£300 for the piece, but he believed that this painting was much more valuable than I suggested and was under the impression that he would attract more buyers and a better price at a London saleroom. He thus declined my suggestion that he sell it outside the capital. At auction, the vendor was proved wrong. His painting sold for £350 – more than my estimate – but illustration charges for the catalogue were £125, the insurance charge was £35 and, of course, there was a commission charge, in this instance, £105, plus VAT. As a result, the vendor came away with less than £100 for his painting.

C IS FOR PATRICK CAULFIELD

What makes art collectable? Is it the skill of the artist, the buyers who flock to collect, or do critics and scholars dictate which paintings, drawings and prints make good investments? Whatever the answer, art has been a passion for people the world over for the past several centuries and beyond.

The works of Patrick Caulfield (1936–2005) are among the most collectable at the moment. His striking silk-screen prints and graphic outlines, which make bold statements and epitomize modern life in many ways, feature in many private and public collections across the globe.

Caulfield studied at Chelsea School of Art from 1956 until 1960. He then moved on to London's prestigious Royal College of Art, returning to Chelsea in 1963, where he taught art until 1971. In 1965 his first exhibition was held at the Friar Gallery in London. It was an instant hit, and Caulfield's international reputation was rapidly established, with numerous one-man exhibitions throughout the world. Among Caulfield's inspirations and influences were some of the greatest modern artists of the 20th century, including Edward Hopper, Mark Rothko, Jackson Pollock and Roy Liechtenstein in particular.

Caulfield started to experiment with printmaking in 1964. Among his early pieces is a silk-screen print called *Ruins*, a striking image that set the standard for his bold style. Caulfield's approach was to document everyday objects in their environment, much like a traditional still life, but with an injection of modern vitality. *Ruins* was

What the Commission Charge Covers

In addition to providing an auction house with a profit, the commission charge goes towards its running costs. These include rent; rates; utilities; telephone bills; advertising; staff; printing, publishing and website costs; and, most importantly, experts. A good auction house will have these professionals on hand to guide you to a price that you are happy with, and to catalogue your lots correctly. Please do not begrudge an auction house its commission – it is money well spent.

exhibited at London's Institute of Contemporary Arts (ICA) in November 1964. In the following year, the British Council chose the piece to represent the country at the 4th Paris Biennale, where it won the unofficial *Prix des Jeunes Artistes* award.

Caulfield did not produce any more silk-screens until 1967, when he discovered a way to present his work on a smaller scale without losing any of the impact. Over the next 25 years, he produced 90 silk-screen prints, all of them fresh, bright and lively. Vivid colours dominate most of the images in a way that makes the artworks unique. Items from everyday life – including jugs, lampshades, wine-glasses, a bathroom mirror, a lamp and a water jug – are brought to the attention of the viewer through Caulfield's use of bold, black lines, which stand out from the often-colourful background and provide a warm feeling of familiarity with the subject.

Patrick Caulfield's silk-screen prints were produced in various sizes as limited editions of 40 to 150 per picture. Each one was signed and numbered by the artist. As with all limited-edition prints, the most desirable and collectable are the early numbers of the run; for example, the first 10 out of 75. The artist proof editions, which are normally marked as such, are especially valuable.

I would certainly advise investing in a Patrick Caulfield print, as they are still relatively cheap for such an important British artist, and I'm certain that they will only go up in value. However, be selective, as the prints must be in top condition, with no tears, stains or signs of fading. Happy hunting.

C IS FOR COINS

Coins provide a delightful insight in to yesteryear. Personally I find it fascinating to think that an antique farthing or a halfpenny was once worth enough to buy a loaf of bread.

Coin collecting is a specialist area. Not long ago it was looked upon as a rich man's hobby, but now many people take great pleasure in collecting coins. Some individuals collect any type of coin, while others specialize in a particular field.

Coin condition is of the utmost importance, as the condition of the coin will always affect its value. There are several grades that you need to be aware of if you are going to collect in this area, as they can tell you much about the condition of a coin. A coin in first-class condition is usually described as *'fleur-de-coin'*, which is normally abbreviated to FDC. This indicates that the coin has not been used, and remains in perfect condition. Another term to look out for is 'mint state', which refers to modern coins that remain in the condition in which they were struck. You may also come across the term 'uncirculated mint condition', which means that the coin has never been used; this term is often applied to 'boxed proof' coins. Next are coins described as 'extremely fine', which is abbreviated to EF. Coins that have this grading show some limited wear. The following grade is 'very fine', which is abbreviated to VF. A coin in this condition is worth adding to a collection, and is worth holding on to until a coin in better condition comes your way. Below very fine comes 'fair or fine', which is abbreviated to FN – coins that are classified with these terms show substantial wear and tear. Finally, there are coins that are classified as 'poor', or P. Once you start to build a collection you will quickly gain an insight into the conditions to look for.

A key factor to bear in mind when collecting coins is rarity. Most coin auctions or catalogues will use one of several 'R' abbreviations to indicate an item's scarcity. A four R rating is the highest indication of rarity and value; a three R rating means a coin is extremely rare; a two R rating indicates that it is very rare; and a single R indicates rare. Other abbreviations that you may also come across are S, which means scarce; N indicating normal; C for common; C2 for very common; and C3, which indicates that a coin is extremely common.

English Coinage

Here are some specific items to look out for if you intend to collect English coins:

GOLD COINS

The £5 coin. This was originally struck as a proof piece during the reign of George III (*r.* 1760–1820), and it has been created occasionally since, usually for coronations or jubilees.

The sovereign, or pound piece. This was first struck in 1817, during the reign of George III. The sovereign was the official unit of English currency and a descendant of the guinea, which was first struck during the reign of Charles II (*r.* 1660–85); it was withdrawn from circulation in 1813.

The £2 gold coin. This was struck as a proof during the reign of George IV (*r.*1820–30), and is sometimes called a double sovereign.

SILVER AND NICKEL COINS

The crown, or five shilling piece. This was first struck in silver in 1551, during the reign of Edward VI (*r.* 1547–53). Although it was commonly used, especially during the reign of Queen Victoria (*r.* 1837–1901), it was last struck in silver in 1937. Thereafter, nickel was used.

The half crown. This was also first struck in silver during the reign of Edward VI; it was manufactured in nickel from 1947.

The florin, or two-shilling piece. This was first struck in 1849, during the reign of Queen Victoria, although the name was applied to gold coins during the reign of Edward III (*r.* 1327–77). From 1947, it was struck in nickel.

The shilling. This was first struck as a silver piece in the reign of Henry VII (*r.* 1485–1509), and has been utilized in every reign every since.

The sixpence. This was first struck in silver in the reign of Edward VI, and has been struck during almost every reign since. It was made in nickel from 1947.

Dealers and Dealing

There are many types of antique dealer, from the part-timer who has the occasional stall at an antiques fair or dabbles on eBay, to the general dealer who has a shop that's open at regular hours and who may occasionally sell goods at large antiques fairs. Then there are the upmarket specialist dealers, who have grand showrooms and exhibit and sell at all the most prestigious fairs. Whatever level they trade at, these dealers all have one thing in common – profit!

So how do you go about becoming an antiques dealer? Whatever level you enter the trade at, as with any business you need to start with a proper financial plan and work out a profitability factor. Most dealers work on the basis of a 100 percent mark-up, which means that if you buy something for £50, you would price it at £100. Sometimes you might price an object at more than 100 percent, to allow customers to haggle and push the price down, which is normal practice in the antique business. Most prices can be negotiated by 10 percent, and sometimes by even more.

The Part-Time Dealer

Let's start on the first rung of the ladder, with the part-time dealer who decides to take a table at an antiques fair. In order to become one, you will first need to accumulate a considerable amount of stock – to make any serious money I would suggest an initial outlay of £3,000–£4,000. You also need to be good at book-keeping, as you will need to keep a stock book, containing details of where you purchased each item and how much you bought and sold it for. Don't forget that you will have to pay tax on any profit you make.

So now you have the money and you're ready to spend it, but what do you buy and where do you buy it? Clearly, an auction house is the best option, but as I keep reiterating, you must research the market, have a good idea of what you are going to buy, study the catalogue in detail and ask lots of questions.

Of course, you need to think about what will attract potential buyers to your stall. If there is one golden rule it has to be this: display well to sell well. If your stand looks attractive and the items on it are in good condition and neatly set out, you are guaranteed the interest of the buyers at the fair. You should also have something on your stall that stands out and attracts customers, perhaps an object that is large, brightly coloured or a unique shape. It is also worth remembering that if you decide to concentrate on a particular area, then specialist collectors will head straight for your stall.

You also need to ensure that your pricing is correct. Remember that you can only price an object correctly if you've bought properly. When you attend auctions, don't be tempted to buy something at £80 with an additional 15 percent buyer's premium if the highest price you can achieve for the item on your stall is £120.

So you have invested your money, rented your plot at the fair and it's time for your first show. But how much can you expect to make? On an average day, you should expect to turn over 10–15 percent of your stock in hand. For example, you should aim to achieve a minimum sales target of £300 to a maximum of £500 (or more) for your £3,000 worth of stock.

Let's imagine you've had an average day and have taken in £400. From this sum, you need to deduct the initial cost to you of the items sold, which will probably be something in the region of £200–£220. Next you need to deduct the cost of the stall, which is usually about £20–£40 per day, and travel costs, say £10. This leaves you with a net profit of approximately £140 – not bad for a day's work! Once you have gained confidence, there is nothing to stop you from doing three or four antiques fairs a month, bearing in mind that you will need to replace any stock you have sold.

D IS FOR ROYAL DOULTON

Royal Doulton is a prolific company that has produced a plethora of items over the 150 or more years that it has been in existence. The company's products have included advertising wares, ashtrays, bookends, character jugs, busts, vases, centrepieces – the list goes on. However, this analysis is going to concentrate on one particular aspect of Royal Doulton: its figurines.

This is a terrific area for collectors. Numerous reference books have been published that aid budding collectors, as they date and price Royal Doulton figurines (see page 156). There are also many collectors' clubs associated with this distinguished brand, and these too are a useful source for information.

Royal Doulton began to produce figurines in 1890, under the guidance of their Art Director, Charles Noke. He commissioned leading sculptors of the period to create designs for Doulton, and these early Noke figurines are the *premier cru* for collectors. A second wave of Royal Doulton figurines was introduced in 1913. Each of these was given a registration number, prefixed by the initials 'HN', which many people think stands for 'house number'. In fact, they are the initials of Harry Nixon, who was Royal Doulton's chief colourist at the time. Ever since, every figurine has carried a HN number, with HN1 a figurine called 'Darling'.

The HN series is still being produced today, and over 3,000 figurine designs have been made since it began. Many designs are now discontinued, and these are now sought-after collectors' items.

The HN range was manufactured in small numbers to start. Between 1913–17 only 680 figures were produced, representing 47 different characters. Like the pieces from Noke's period, these figurines are also among the desirable.

During the 1920s several new figures were added to the series, and production began to expand as its popularity grew. In the 1940s, 409 figurine designs were withdrawn; only 2,000 of each of these models are believed to have been produced. It is no surprise that the figurines that have survived from this period command top prices.

Despite the great volume of Royal Doulton figurines that have been produced over the years, they have become very popular collector's items. But it was not until the early 1970s that collecting Royal Doulton really gathered momentum, when a book called *Royal Doulton Figurines* was produced, listing all the items available at that time. It continues to be an invaluable guide for collectors of the brand.

When collecting Royal Doulton figurines, you need to be aware of the rarity of the figure and the different colourways and variations that exist within each design. Many figurines, particularly those from the 'Lady' series, were produced in several colour variations. For example, 'Victorian Lady' is known to exist in 15 different colourways. Sometimes colourways that have never been recorded before turn up. It's extremely difficult to value an object like this, but if you do find one you can probably expect it to fetch at least 100 percent more than a common colour scheme.

When investing in Royal Doulton figurines, certain factors need to be taken into consideration. If you are buying to sell a figure on, you need to be aware that most collectors will be armed with books, and are well aware of the current retail prices. If you are buying to build your own collection, my advice is to buy wisely and only purchase items that are in perfect condition. Once you have gained in knowledge and feel confident with your purchasing skills, I recommend that you attend auctions, as you will find that some figurines sell for a lot less in the saleroom than they do at antiques fairs.

Examples of Royal Doulton figurines from the 1990s include the 'Snowman' series, which retailed in the late 1990s at prices of £10–£20. The figures were based on the phenomenally successful animated film *The Snowman*. Sadly, they were not a great hit for Royal Doulton, and so some of the figurines were produced on a smaller scale, but this just makes these figurines more collectable. Just over 10 years later some of these figures are commanding £100–£200.

There are a few things worth noting before you set up your stall:

• Not every antiques fair will be busy, so you might not make a profit every time.

• The best time to rent an indoor stall is from September until May. People tend to visit indoor antiques fairs more frequently in the winter.

• To maximize your profits throughout the year, I recommend that you attend fairs that take place outside from May to September.

• When you rent a stall at an antiques fair you gain early access to the event, which gives you a chance to look around and perhaps find yourself a bargain – many items change hands before the public even arrives.

A Shop of your Own

The next step up from a stall at an antiques fair is a shop. This will obviously allow you more space to display your items. It will also provide a permanent base, so that specialist collectors you have become acquainted with know where to find you. The overheads for a set-up like this are obviously going to be a lot more expensive than the occasional stall. The outlay on stock will also have to be increased to cover the additional expenses a permanent property would involve. Once again, your target should be a turnover of between 10–20 percent of the stock in hand. Although profit margins can be higher if you have a retail unit, it is a very big, not to mention brave, step to make, and you seriously need to know your stuff before taking on this sort of business venture. If you fancy moving up in the antiques business, I highly recommend that you do a year's apprenticeship in and around fairs and auction rooms to get a feel for the lots and prices before taking on a shop.

General Dealers

A general dealer is an individual who has a warehouse or similar storage unit, or a retail outlet in which to display their wares. This type of dealer does not specialize in any particular area, but buys goods purely for profit. I have witnessed this type of dealer many times in auction rooms; they usually buy anything – furniture, silver, china and paintings – as long as it is visually attractive and they can turn it over for a quick profit. These dealers need to be extremely hard-working and they're often quite successful because of the long hours they put in. I know some general dealers who work twelve hours a day, seven days a week. Like anybody, they are capable of making mistakes, but they don't often lose money. A general dealer will often pack a van with items that he or she hasn't been able to sell, and will offload the goods at a large fair for a smaller profit, sometimes even taking a small loss.

Dealing on the Internet

Let's not forget the new brand of dealers: the ones that operate on eBay. This website has proved a phenomenon in the collecting world, and its impact increases daily. On eBay you can sell anything – from a cheap electric fan to a Picasso painting. You need to set aside quite a lot of time to photograph your items and list them for the website, however, and you'll have to package and transport anything you sell.

The process is quite simple. Your items are listed on the website, and a 3-, 7- or 10-day limit for bids is allocated. eBay charges you a commission if you sell the items, and a listing fee whether they sell or not. This site is also an excellent reference point if you want to check out current prices and explore sales trends. Most of the eBay dealers I know tend to specialize in areas such as books, Royal Doulton, Wade pottery, cigarette cards, postcards or ephemera. Dealing in smaller items makes it easier to send the goods to buyers. Selling this way can be very profitable; I know several people who make a decent living from selling antiques and collectables on eBay. It's certainly a site worth visiting if you are interested in antiques. (For more on this subject, see pages 88–89.)

Whatever route you decide to take to become a dealer, I wish you luck. I guarantee that you will have fun along the way, learn a lot, meet some interesting characters and make good friends en route.

D IS FOR DAVID SHARP

David Sharp of Rye pottery is fast becoming one of the most collectable potters of the 20th century. His diverse range of pots, figurines and moneyboxes, most of which have minimal hand-painted decoration, make them very desirable. The Americans are currently collecting David Sharp pottery as fast as it comes to the market. Examples from the 1950s and 1960s can still be had for £20–£30. Large pieces, especially the animal figures, can reach over £100.

Estimates

Estimates appear in most auction catalogues, but what are they for? Are they for the benefit of the buyer, the seller or the auctioneer? In fact, they are for the benefit of everyone, and they also provide a basic guide-line showing the price range that the vendors and auction house would be happy to achieve in the sale. Sometimes estimates are based around the reserve price (see pages 94–95), which is usually 10 percent less than the lowest estimate.

Most catalogue estimates contain low and high estimates, although these often seem irrelevant when items come under the hammer. On several occasions, I have given a lot an estimate of, say, £200–£300, only for the item to reach £1,500, something that is not uncommon in sale-rooms. Only recently I saw a catalogue estimate of £150–£250 for an early-20th-century amphora vase. A similar item had sold for £2,500 just four weeks previously, so I asked myself how the auctioneer had arrived at this low number. It was simply because the owner was content for the item to be sold within that guide price. The item went on to make £2,900, which made the auctioneer happy, as it meant more commission for the saleroom. The owner was also extremely content, given that he was only expecting £250!

Situations like this happen daily at auctions, and most auctioneers will tell you that a low estimate actually attracts more buyers into the saleroom – the trade calls this a 'come-and-buy-me estimate'. This phenomenon is quite understandable, because if you think about it, it makes far more sense to have four people bidding on an item than a

ABOVE: Always be sure to inspect every aspect of an object and look carefully at detailing such as marquetry.
BELOW: Particularly important is checking whether an object's fittings are original and still in sound order.

PLATE 1

ABOVE: Checking a drawer for replacement handles, cracks or splinters in the wood or infestation.

BELOW: A set of collectables is more valuable than a single item in a genre and, accordingly, will typically command a higher price at auction.

PLATE 2

ABOVE: The auctioneer will identify the highest bidder in the audience, so everyone will know whom he or she is now bidding against.
BELOW: The showing of a bidder's number card or catalogue, or simply a raised hand, is all an auctioneer needs in order to know a bidder's intentions.

PLATE 3

ABOVE: Don't be afraid to take lots off a wall (with care, of course!) to allow closer inspection.

BELOW: Jigsaws can be very collectable. This scarce example of the GWR 'Night Mail' was made by Chad Valley in the 1930s and still has its original box.

PLATE 4

ABOVE: Children's toys and books have risen greatly in value recently. Good-quality pop-up books like this 1930s Children's Annual are much sought-after. *BELOW:* Antiquarian and secondhand bookstores often have a good stock of fascinating reference books on antiques and collecting.

PLATE 5

ABOVE AND LEFT: Using a spy-glass is easy and absolutely crucial when dating silver or gold hallmarks. It is worth practising at home until you feel confident and comfortable using one.

OPPOSITE: Job lots are always worth a look. You never know what might be tucked away at the bottom!

PLATE 6

PLATE 7

ABOVE: This 1930s Royal Albert coffee set with the 'Lido' pattern is typical of its period and of great interest to Art Deco enthusiasts.
BELOW: A tip for the future: 1960s coffee sets like this Lord Nelson 'Serenade' design are commanding higher prices but are still affordable, so buy now!

PLATE 8

single individual bidding against a high reserve price.

At some auctions, the lots are not allocated estimates. This normally suggests that the item does not have a reserve on it, and is valued at less than £50 by the auctioneer (although in some London salerooms I have seen this happen with items under £200).

Most salerooms will not reveal the reserve price on lots entered into their sales, as this is a confidential matter between the selling client and the auctioneer. The auctioneer is rather like a middleman between the seller and the bidders, and he is a confidant as well. The maintenance of confidentiality on behalf of both buyers and sellers is of paramount importance: the buyer may not want other buyers to know that he or she is bidding, and the seller may not want the buyer to know that he or she owns the lot, as he or she may be also be bidding on it.

It is extremely rare for an auctioneer to reveal details of buyers and sellers. However, on several occasions I have been approached by buyers who have missed the lot they are interested in and have come to me in an attempt to contact the successful bidder and make a further offer on the lot. When this happens, I contact the buyer on their behalf and ask if they would like to be contacted by another prospective buyer. Nine times out of ten, they do not. That said, if you do miss out on a lot it is always worth having this sort of chat with the auctioneer.

Everyone should be aware of the extra costs that they might incur

E IS FOR EERO SAARINEN

After studying art for a year, Eero Saarinen (1910–61) decided to become an architect. He also turned his hand to furniture, some of which turns up at 20th-century design sales, where it is hugely popular. One of the most iconic of the Finnish designer's works is the 'Tulip' chair and table, which dates from the mid-1950s. These sold cheaply in their day, but you can expect to pay over £1,000 for an original set today. There are also reproductions around that you can pick up for a couple of hundred pounds. Saarinen, who is one of my personal favourites, also produced such iconic chairs as the 'Grasshopper' model no. 61, which dates from 1946–47, and the 'Womb' chair, which dates to the late 1940s. Most of the designs carry the trademark of Knoll Associates.

E IS FOR EAMES

Charles (1907–78) and Ray (1925–88) Eames were an American couple who formed one of the most dynamic and multi-talented design partnerships of the 20th century. Their work is now highly sought after by collectors of modern work, and the sheer scope and range of their designs is incredible, including architecture, furniture, textiles and even toys.

The Eames were described by their friends as humanitarian, witty and charming. What they desired most from their designs was that they should be enjoyed as part of a lifestyle.

Just 40 furniture designs were produced by the Eames Office, production ending with Charles's death in 1978. He was inspired by the work of the Finnish designer Alvar Aalto (1894–1949) and the legendary American architect Frank Lloyd Wright (1869–1959). Passionate about both these designers' love of organic forms, Charles was also intrigued by Aalto's experimental work with moulded plywood furniture. He originally studied architecture at Washington University, eventually moving to Michigan's prestigious Cranbrook Academy of Art. Here he went on to become head of the college's design department, where he met Ray Kaiser – the couple married in 1941.

Charles first came to public attention in 1940, when a chair he had designed won an award at an organic furniture competition run by the Museum of Modern Art in New York. In 1941 he and Ray moved to California, where they started their first commercial enterprise, producing plywood leg splints and stretchers for the American Navy. By 1942 Ray was experimenting with plywood, producing sculptured chairs that demonstrated her interest in the Avant Garde movement.

The couple's first major project together was the design of their own house, which was built in California between 1945 and 1949. It was part of the Case Study movement in the US, which encouraged architects and designers to create high-quality, well-designed houses for the postwar period. It is a perfect example of an economically built, well-thought-out space for living and working, reflecting the Modernist ideas that were first voiced by the Bauhaus movement earlier in the 20th century. The interior relates perfectly to the exterior, with complete co-ordination throughout. The Eames House is a true architectural masterpiece.

By the mid-1940s, production of their designs was moving forward, with everything from children's chairs and room dividers to ten-panel screens and stools. In 1946, the same year that the large furniture company Herman Miller took over the marketing of the Eames' designs, Charles created a masterpiece: a lounge chair and ottoman that comprised a three-piece moulded shell and leather upholstery. Ten thousand of these chairs were sold, and original examples of the design are much desired by collectors today.

Such was the success of the couple's designs that Herman Miller also took over the manufacture of Eames furniture in 1948. By the 1950s they were using fibreglass, designing tables and chairs with immense confidence. One moulded fibreglass seat, which sat on a wire base, is known in the trade as the 'cat's cradle' or the 'Eiffel chair'. Original examples have a white, black-and-red chequer label under the chair that bears the words Miller and Zenith. Examples of this chair are extremely sought after by collectors. In 1958, the couple produced the Aluminium Group chairs. Instantly recognizable, they have a swivel base with leather or upholstered seating.

The price of the couple's furniture continues to rise. Ten years ago, an Eames chair could be purchased for a few hundred pounds. Today they are anything upwards of £4,000, with rare pieces fetching £6,000. However, I would still recommend that you buy furniture designed by the Eameses, as they are timeless items and make a very sound investment, with the added advantage that they are extremely comfortable. I speak from experience, as my office chair is an Eames original; I have owned it for many years and would never be tempted to sell it.

One thing to bear in mind when buying furniture designed by the Eameses is that a company called Vitra were given the licence to produce the couple's designs in Europe. They continue to do so today, their items bearing a facsimile of Charles Eames's signature.

E IS FOR EROTICA

Art of an erotic nature – usually known as erotica – is a vast subject, and when quality items do show up in salerooms they attract a good deal of interest. This means that prices tend to be high!

The period from the late-19th-century to the 1950s is extremely popular, as there were some great artists working at this time. Personal favourites include works by Louis Icart (1888–1950) and Aubrey Beardsley (1872–98). From a slightly earlier period, original prints by Thomas Rowlandson (1756–1827) can still be found, but be warned, as there are also many reproduction prints in circulation.

There were some superb bronzes of partially clad women produced from early in the 20th century through to the 1930s. These can fetch tens of thousands of pounds in salerooms, particularly if they were created by the top Art Deco artists, for example, Bruno Zack or Louis Chalon. The French designer René Lalique (1860–1945) also produced some stunning examples of erotic art.

However, there is one aspect of erotica that I believe still has plenty of mileage in it. Pin-up magazines, particularly those from the 1950s and 1960s, are likely to yield healthy profits in years to come. It's certainly worth looking out for publications that contain spreads featuring icons like Marilyn Monroe or other famous models of the period.

when buying or selling antiques. Most of these extra charges occur when selling. For example, on top of the commission levied by the auction house, there might also be a lottage fee. This ranges anywhere from £1 to £10, depending on the auction house, and generally covers the auctioneer's costs of cataloguing the item, moving it around the saleroom and unloading it when it is being delivered by the transport team.

You also need to be aware of packing and transport costs. The auction house needs to pass on any such costs to you, and so before you instruct an auction room to collect your goods you should ask what the cost will be. Other charges come in the form of insurance, normally charged from between one and two percent of the hammer price. Most auction houses offer the option on whether or not you wish to insure your items whilst they are in the saleroom, but bear in mind that your items may already be insured under your household policy. A quick phone call to your insurance company will set you straight and could save you money.

Watch out also for illustration charges in auction catalogues. These should be pointed out to you before the lots are illustrated, but beware: they can be as much as £500 for a full-page glossy colour illustration. Are they worth this money? I speak from experience when I say that producing a nice, glossy coloured catalogue really does make a difference. Many clients are immediately drawn to illustrated items; indeed, without photographs of the more stunning lots most dealers will flip through a catalogue and might miss them altogether. Where do you draw the line on what to illustrate and what not to illustrate? My advice would be to think along the following lines when you are considering illustrations:

Consider the value of the item concerned. If it is below £300 then it is not worth illustrating. If over £500, then try to negotiate a price. If your items are worth over £5,000, then you are in a strong negotiating position, not only for the illustration charges but also for the rate of commission. Also think carefully if you have a rare or unusual item to sell. Illustrations are defiantly worthwhile in such cases. Over the years I have recommended to clients that they illustrate a rare item (even of small worth) purely on its scarcity value. Although the auction house guide may be quite low, the rarity of this item would make it hard to put a fixed price when it comes to reserve or estimates. In the auction trade we call this a 'come-and-buy-me estimate'. Illustrating such a lot like this will increase the number of collectors who become intrigued and wish to bid on it.

To sum up, extra charges might include transport, lottage and illustrations, but there is one other cost which auction rooms might hit you with and one with which I personally disagree. This is the 'unsold lot' fee, which can range from £5 per lot to 10 percent of the lower estimate. To my mind, if a lot remains unsold the auction house has either got the estimate wrong or has not attracted enough – or the right sort of – customers to the sale. I strongly recommend therefore that before your goods go to the auction house you talk to the staff and check whether they operate an unsold lot fee system. If this is the case, I urge you to find an auction room that does not charge this fee!

Fakes and Forgeries

Fake and forgery are two words that are often heard in the antiques world, along with terms like copy, reproduction, replica, facsimile, counterfeit and attribution. Unfortunately, there is no rule of thumb for detecting a fake or a forgery, but recognizing an object that follows either description becomes easier with experience, and ensuring that you're an expert in your field makes a world of difference. Fakes and forgeries are an occupational hazard in the world of antiques and collectables, and almost everyone I know in the trade has been tricked at least once.

Let me explain the distinction between the two terms. A fake is any work of art or object that has been created or altered to look as if it is older or more valuable than it really is. A forgery is an item that is constructed as a deliberate imitation of a specific object. A forgery is not the same as a copy or an imitation. A copy does not claim to be an original or contain fake marks, dates or signatures. For example, if an artist attempted to reproduce John Constable's painting *The Haywain*, but signed it with his own name, the end result is obviously a copy. However, if they painstakingly replicate the painting's every detail and sign the painting 'John Constable' then the work becomes a forgery.

It would be impossible for me to describe the many different clues to look out for in order to identify fakes and forgeries when venturing into the world of antiques. I can, however, say that you are relatively safe if you visit an established auction room, as most catalogue descriptions will

F IS FOR FARMING EQUIPMENT

I must be honest and say that this is quite a quirky field in which to collect and the value of old farming equipment is really dependant on its decorative potential. Farming equipment can be picked up cheaply at some country sales and it will look fantastic in your back garden as ornamental pieces. Many of the 19th-century items have a particularly aesthetic appeal. Smaller items, for example, Victorian cast iron farm scales and 19th-century sheep shearers, can be picked up for under £20. The most sought-after items include plough machines and cultivators with wooden wagons. All in all, this is a good area in which to collect if you fancy having an interesting garden.

highlight whether or not the item is a genuine antique or a copy. To read between the lines of these descriptions and understand the many terms used, you need to consult the glossary, which is usually found at the back or front of an auction catalogue.

How to Read a Catalogue Description

I cannot stress enough how important it is to understand what an auctioneer is telling you in a catalogue. When you look through these publications, there are several things to look out for, particularly if you are intending to buy art. Here's a quick guide to deciphering some of the points you will come across in the auctioneer's descriptions.

1. If the first name and surname of the artist are listed, this means that the work is, in the auctioneer's opinion, a genuine work by that individual.
2. If the catalogue description displays the artist's first name initial, along with the surname, the auctioneer is telling you that he or she believes the work is of the period in which the artist flourished, and is at least partly, if not entirely, the artist's work.
3. If the catalogue shows only the surname of the artist, it is the opinion of the auction house that the work is from the same school as the artist and was done by one of his or her followers.
4. If the catalogue description reads 'after', followed by the artist's surname, it is, in the opinion of the auctioneer, a copy.

5. You may also come across the term 'bears signature' or 'traces of signature' – this means that, in the auctioneer's opinion, despite the presence of a signature, it cannot be verified that the work is actually by the artist.

F IS FOR FAMOUS FORGER

Tom Keating (1918–84) was a notorious character who claimed to have forged over 2,000 paintings by over 100 different artists. A true Cockney, Keating was born in London to a poor family. After the Second World War, he began to restore paintings for a living, and also worked as a decorator to make ends meet. He also had ambitions as an artist in his own right and exhibited his work, yet had little success.

Keating firmly believed that the art world was crooked, and that critics and dealers connived to line their own pockets at the expense of naive collectors and impoverished artists. He decided to fight back, creating forgeries and hoping to destabilize the art market and the system that governed it.

Keating planted 'time-bombs' in his creations, leaving clues to the paintings' true nature for fellow art restorers or experts to find. For example, he sometimes wrote on the blank canvas, knowing that once he had painted over it, only X-rays could reveal the text. He deliberately added flaws and used materials peculiar to the 20th century.

His favourite artist was Rembrandt. To create a 'Rembrandt', he manufactured pigments by boiling nuts for ten hours, filtering the result through silk. A colouring of this nature eventually fades, unlike the earth pigments used by the real artist. As an art restorer, Keating knew about the chemistry of cleaning fluids, so a layer of glycerine under a layer of paint ensured that when his forged paintings were cleaned, as all oil paintings need to be eventually, the glycerine would dissolve, the paint layer would disintegrate and the painting – now a ruin – would reveal itself as a fake.

Occasionally, Keating came across frames with old catalogue numbers from Christie's, the renowned auction house. These inch-high stencilled black letters and numbers helped him to establish false provenances for his forgeries. He would call the auction room to ask whose paintings the frames had contained, before

6. Yet another term to look out for is 'antique style', which means the item depicted is of no great age, but is based on an original antique. If you are serious about collecting and intend to invest in antiques, ensure that you invest in originals.

painting the pictures in the artist's style.

Keating produced a number of watercolours in the style of the English Romantic painter Samuel Palmer (1805–81). In 1970, auctioneers noticed that 13 of Palmer's watercolours were for sale, all of them depicting the same theme, the rural village of Shoreham in Kent. When an article in *The Times* voiced suspicions about the origin of these works, Keating confessed that he had painted them all. He also estimated that more than 2,000 of his forgeries were in circulation. He had created them, he declared, as a protest against all the traders that get rich at the expense of artists. He refused to list the forgeries he had produced.

Keating was arrested in 1977 and accused of conspiracy to defraud, however the case against him was dropped because of his bad health. Stress, combined with years of smoking and inhaling fumes from the chemicals used in art restoration, had taken its toll. But Keating rallied and, although increasingly fragile, he presented television programmes in 1982–83 that explored the techniques of the Old Masters.

In 1983, Keating stated that, in his opinion, he was not an especially good painter. His proponents would disagree. Even when he was alive, many celebrity collectors, including the ex-heavyweight boxer, Henry Cooper, began to collect Keating's work. After his death in 1984, his paintings became increasingly valuable to collectors. Ironically, Christie's, the auction house that had inadvertently helped Keating with his deception, sold 204 of his paintings that same year. I attended the sale and was astonished by the sheer volume of his works. Even his known forgeries, described in catalogues as being 'after' Gainsborough or Cézanne, attain high prices, as do his signed works. A painting by Keating can make anything from £500 to £5,000 at auction. I wonder what he would think about that if he were still alive today.

Good Investments

Many people do not look for a profit when buying antiques for their home, and yet, like the stock market and property, antiques and fine art have proved to be good investments over the years. Most antiques tend to increase in value by at least 5–10 percent annually. However, is worth noting that, like the stock market, the world of antiques has its peaks and troughs. But what is a good investment, and when should you take the plunge and make one?

Investments can vary in size and, of course, they depend on your budget and whether you want to invest individually or as part of a group. Businesses are not immune to investing in antiques. One example of this is the British Rail board, which invested part of its pension fund in fine art, concentrating on paintings by well-known listed artists. The company employed experts to source the paintings and bought them through auction houses and from museums. After a period of years, these items were sold for an impressive profit.

What's Made Money

Knowing what to invest in is tricky, of course, but it is often worth the risk. Moorcroft pottery is a good example of how a collectable can prove to be a good investment (see pages 78–79). This prolific company was founded in the late 1890s by William and Walter Moorcroft; it has produced some fine examples over the years, and continues to do so. Today, the Moorcroft factory makes reproductions of some of its older examples as limited editions for collectors. The original pottery became fashion-able in auction rooms in the 1970s, when items bearing the Moorcroft stamp could be bought from £10–£100. If you were lucky enough to have bought these pieces then, I guarantee you would make a profit from your investment today that would far exceed your £10 or £100 remain-ing in the bank.

Another category that has proved profitable, and may continue to do so, is English furniture from the 18th century. This covers a huge price range, from £500–£50,000. When buying this sort of item you must be very confident and research the subject properly, or employ a reliable advisor; many specialist antique dealers will buy on your behalf for a commission.

Predicting Trends

Ideally, one wants to predict what is going to be the next trend in antiques and buy now before it peaks. If you are going to do this, you need to keep your finger on the pulse, staying aware of what's happen-ing in salerooms and reading trade magazines, as this will help highlight those items that are starting to increase in value.

I have had a bit of luck with this myself, as in the early 1980s my wife and I began to collect Poole pottery's 'Delphis' range, which dates to the 1960s and 1970s. The items are very bright, and display vivid colours. At the time, pieces from this range were extremely easy to find at antiques fairs, fetching between £2–£30, depending on size. In 2005, that £2 fetched £20, and £30 could see a return of £300.

Another range that has proved profitable is Troika pottery, a Cornish make that was produced from 1963 and features strong geometric designs. In the 1980s it was unheard of for a piece of Troika pottery to make £100 in a sale, yet today almost any piece will make that amount.

What to Invest in Now

What and how much you invest will obviously reflect the return you expect to receive. If you buy an antique for investment, you need to bear in mind that you will have to keep hold of it for a few years before it will show a return, so make sure when you buy something that you can live with it for a while!

You also need to have a comprehensive knowledge of what you are investing in before taking the plunge. If you are looking to invest in something that will show you a profit, then there are a few areas of antiques that I would recommend.

One period that is amenable to most budgets is the 'Swinging Sixties'. This period represents one of the peaks in British culture, with pop music, fashion, sport and technology – think Concorde – all on a high. Anything that relates to the England football team winning the World Cup in 1966 is very collectable, but condition is all-important, and if the item, for example a World Cup Willie doll, is boxed, then the box needs to be intact.

When it comes to pop music collectables from the 1960s, I recommend that you look out for psychedelic album covers and rare albums. Often it is the cover artwork and not the record itself that is worth the money. LPs and EPs by the Beatles and the Rolling Stones are already making money, along with those of other famous groups and solo artists from this period.

Film posters from this era have also become collectable, and are worth looking out for; popular examples include *From Russia with Love*, which starred Sean Connery, and *Carry on Camping*.

Some of the toys from this period are also becoming extremely collectable. 'Action Man' reached Britain in 1966, while other dolls of the period include 'Barbie' and 'Sindy'. Many of these are highly sought after, and as such, they are becoming increasingly difficult to find boxed and in good condition. But keep digging, as there are still some out there at boot fairs and in job lots at auction rooms.

Objects produced in the 1970s are also gaining in popularity at the moment. When buying items from this period, you need to get hold of articles that epitomize the decade. One item to look out for is the Trimphone, which was first launched in 1975 with a dial. In 1977 a push-button edition of the Trimphone came out. Both models are collectable. Another gadget that is increasing in value is the famous Stylophone, which came to prominence in the late 1960s and 1970s, and was promoted by Rolf Harris.

Let's not forget the change to decimal currency, which occurred on February 15, 1971. Many households have a boxed set of the first decimal coins, and the memorabilia bought out when decimalization was introduced is definitely worth a look.

From the realm of fashion, keep your eyes peeled for items by the top designers of the time, for example Mary Quant and Vivienne Westwood. And don't forget those platform shoes.

Pop music also had its moments in the 1970s, with teeny-boppers like

G IS FOR GARDEN GNOMES

I am a great believer in accumulating items that are fun to collect and form great conversation pieces, and garden gnomes certainly fall into this category. The idea of magical little people dates from early mythology. Garden gnomes were traditionally believed to have guarded the treasures of the inner Earth, and this is perhaps why so many of them have been produced over the years.

If you want to collect at the top end of the market, the best gnomes to look out for are early examples, which are carved out of hardwood or stone. Early-20th-century gnomes are also collectable, especially objects from the 1930s, 1940s and 1950s, which are usually seated or standing in comical poses.

More common examples can be picked up for anything between £10–£40, although gnomes with glass eyes are a bit more expensive at £50–£100. Gnomes from the Victorian period are priced between £100–£500, depending on their size.

David Cassidy, the Jackson Five, the Osmonds and the Bay City Rollers all popular; memorabilia surrounding these groups is worth picking up, but some of the most sought-after pop memorabilia relates to the Sex Pistols. This notorious punk group burst onto the scene in 1975, and was originally formed to publicize Vivienne Westwood's clothes.

These are just a few of the items that might be of interest of you as collectables. Most of them are now relatively cheap, but I feel sure they will only go up in price in the years to come. To help you justify what you pay for an item I would recommend that you think about its rarity value. If an item was mass-produced, it will have little value, but if an item is part of a limited edition, this will enhance its price.

Haggling and Bartering

Haggling and bartering are age-old practices that have been used for centuries. Both tactics are used to negotiate in the antiques trade, and if you know how to ask the right questions you will be able to push down prices. The first piece of advice I would give when attempting to negotiate a price is to be polite. If you approach traders like a bull in a china shop, you'll put them on the defensive immediately and they won't even begin to negotiate with you. If, on the other hand, you approach them in a warm and friendly manner, the chances are that you will definitely be able to negotiate. It is common knowledge that buyers can negotiate a 10 percent reduction on the asking price, but if you haggle properly you may knock off even more.

So where do you begin? Let's say you've seen a Victorian chaise longue that you think would look stunning in your home. The price tag displays £1,500, but there are certain things you need to consider when you read this. First, how much did the dealer pay for it? And second, how much time and money has he spent restoring it to showroom condition?

In my experience, most antiques dealers have a mark-up of at least 50 percent. So if this dealer paid £750 for the chaise longue, then he will make £750 if he gets full price. However, that is not all profit, as he will have to pay tax and VAT, which will reduce the figure to about £500. If he then knocks 10 percent, or £150, off of the asking price, he is down to a £350 net profit.

The first thing you should do is to speak with the dealer to see whether or not you will be able to approach him with an even lower offer. There are also a few questions you need to ask before you proceed, which will help you to decide what sort of offer you can make.

- How long has the item been in stock?
- Has it been fully restored?
- Is the upholstery original?

If, say, the dealer has had the item for six months, and it has been re-upholstered and fully restored, he's unlikely to go beyond the common 10 percent discount, as he has put a large investment into the item.

When you open negotiations, you should begin by targeting the ticket price. With the 10 percent discount, the price of the piece comes down to £1,350. Start off with an offer of £1,200, which suggests that this is what you are willing to pay, and see if the dealer accepts it. If he declines, ask what the best price would be. The dealer may come back with a figure of £1,300. The next question you need to ask is if the price would be any different for cash. You will be amazed at just how many dealers prefer cash over credit cards, mainly as cards carry a two percent surcharge, which is transferred to the customer. The dealer also has to pay the credit card company for the facilities to take cards. For cash, he takes off another £50. You agree. So, after a bit of haggling, the chaise longue, which was priced at £1,500 when you walked into the shop, is going to be yours at £1,250. You have saved £250 – there are not many retail units you can visit to make that sort of deal!

Things are a little different at antiques fairs, as dealers at these events

H IS FOR HEPPLEWHITE FURNITURE

When I say Hepplewhite, I mean the original stuff – not the reproductions that were produced throughout the 19th and 20th centuries. However, investing in original 18th-century Hepplewhite furniture is not a cheap occupation, and you need to ensure that you buy from a bona fide, registered antiques dealer or auction room. Hepplewhite furniture has proved to be a cracking investment over the years, and usually increases in price by as much as eight percent a year. Sets of chairs seem to command a premium.

H IS FOR HOME TERRITORY

Home territory is one of the best ways to start making money in the antiques trade, as it is simple, easy and can be very profitable. But what is it?

It is relatively simple to acquire knowledge of the concept of 'home territory', which involves buying lots specific to a region outside of that area and re-selling them in the place where they are popular. For example, say you are in your local saleroom, which is situated on the south coast, and you discover that your local auctioneer has cleared out the estate of a deceased family from Worcestershire. Among the items in the sale are numerous books about Worcester, a 30-hour Worcester longcase clock and some first-period blue-and-white Worcester pottery. By logging on to the website of an auction house in the Worcester area, you will be able to see what they have sold over the past year – the chances are that items similar to those at the sale you're attending will appear in their catalogue. You could also phone the auction house and find out what prices they are getting for these sorts of Worcester items. Say, for example, that the clock has an estimate of £400–£600 in your local saleroom, but a quick chat with an auctioneer in Worcester informs you that the clock could make as much as £800–£1,200 on home territory. The Worcester books

tend to work for a smaller profit margin, possibly 30–40 percent. However, similar haggling tactics can be used. Ask the same questions as above and work out how much you think you can shave off the asking price. One thing you can consider when making your offer is that the dealer will have set up the stall very early in the morning and would probably prefer not to have to pack every item back up again – the more he sells, the lighter his van will be at the end of the day. In this scenario there is the possibility that the dealer will take a lower price for an object as large as a chaise longue to save him lugging it around again. Cheaper, smaller items that are easily packed up at the end of the day are going to be harder to negotiate on.

It is also a good idea to start buying at the end of the fair. If it is a week-long event, the trader will be keen to sell his stock so that he can replace it with fresh items for the next fair. As an auctioneer, I know this estimated at £10–£20 in your saleroom could make £50–£70 in Worcester. Finally, you discover that a Worcester tea bowl, which is estimated at £50–£80 on the south coast, would make £300–£500 in its home town.

Next, you need to bid on the lots in your local saleroom, before taking them up to Worcester to sell them at a profit. Don't forget that you'll have to pay the buyer's premium when buying the lots, and commission charges when you sell them. It's worth negotiating the charges before you buy the lots, as this will help you to decide what price you want to pay, and also which objects you'll need to secure for a chance at making a profit in Worcester.

By being aware of the 'home territory' market, you can make a quick profit, particularly if you don't mind travelling from one saleroom to another. (I know of one individual who bid on a framed and glazed watercolour of Folkestone Harbour in Scotland, paying £40. By putting it in the right saleroom on the south coast, he made £300.) Furthermore, home territory is definitely an angle you should consider if you want to become a general antiques dealer. As always, my advice is to have knowledge of the items you are buying, as condition, alterations and restoration will all affect the price.

to be true, as while working on the television programme *Bargain Hunt*, I had to trawl around antiques fairs with my teams and try to negotiate the best possible price. Some people believe that traders do special deals when we're making the programme, but believe me we have to haggle just as hard, if not harder! I also appreciate how hard these traders work, so never begrudge them a profit.

If I spot something I fancy when scanning an antiques stall, I try to look at the price tag without the dealer seeing me. If it is priced at £100 I will ask something like 'how much change would I get out of £70 if I bought this?'

By asking this, I've immediately suggested that this is how much I think the item is worth. Nine times out of ten, I'll get the £100 item for £75. Have a go next time you visit an antiques fair – you may just get a positive result.

Insurance and Inspection

Insurance is an incredibly important aspect when dealing with antiques. Any objects that you own with a value of about £500 or more should be insured, for all sorts of reasons, not least of which are fire, burglary and flood damage. The peace of mind you will get by knowing that your precious antiques or collectables are properly insured will keep you securely in the comfort zone.

Some companies will insist on proof of purchase before insuring individual objects. This is usually impossible if you have inherited the item (or items), and that's when you need to call on a professional valuer. They will supply you with a written valuation, outlining the replacement value of each object. Many valuers will also offer to illustrate your valuation with photographs of the item.

Charges For Insurance Valuations

The cost of valuations varies from firm to firm, but the following charges are typical:

• Travel time or consultation charge: £40–£75 per hour, normally at a minimum of one hour.

• Valuation charges: 2 percent for the first £5,000; 1.5 percent up to £25,000; 1 percent thereafter.

Because the charges can vary, it's always best to do some research and compare a few companies before you go ahead with a valuation.

58

Items that are valued at over £1,500 usually need to be mentioned separately on any insurance policy, and there is often an extra premium to pay for such things. It is worth shopping around, as some insurance companies offer a better deal than others. If you are lucky enough to own many valuable antiques, there are specialist insurance companies that will cater for you. These companies tend to offer a comprehensive – and sometimes cheaper – service than a standard insurance company.

Inspecting Items

Inspecting lots before you bid on them is absolutely paramount, but how do you go about this? With any luck, by the time you're ready to start attending auctions, you will have a good understanding of the antiques you wish to buy. As general rule you should use the guidelines that follow when inspecting items you wish to buy.

Assessing Furniture

When you select a piece of furniture you wish to bid on, the first thing you must do is stand back from the item and check that it holds up well. Make sure that it looks in proportion, and that it is has the correct perspective. If you are happy on both these counts, then you need to take a closer look at the item. If, for instance, it is a chest of drawers, open every drawer and make sure that each one fits well and slides properly on its runners. Look inside to see if any of the drawers or runners have been replaced, and check for signs of woodworm.

If the furniture is arranged in lines in the saleroom and you find it difficult to look at an item properly, ask a porter to pull the piece of furniture out to a space where you can assess it in detail. You need to have the opportunity to see if the back has been replaced or has any problems. If the item of furniture has legs or feet, make sure that you check them for any signs of repair.

Two-piece furniture items, for example bureau bookcases, linen presses and chests-on-chests, will almost certainly need close examination. You need to ensure that both pieces match, and that they are not just a marriage of convenience. The best way to do this is to stand back from the item and look at the grain of the wood, checking to see if it matches throughout the piece from top to bottom. Also, take a look at the sides of the object and make sure the wood grain matches here as well. In the case of a bureau bookcase, there are telltale signs that indicate if the item is a 'marriage': the bureau base and the bookcase on top of it should fit together perfectly and be in perfect proportion. One of most effective ways of ascertaining whether an item has been made from two different pieces is to look at the back of it. Both the top and bottom should look exactly the same. All of the items mentioned above are expensive to buy at auction, so if you are thinking of investing in pieces like this then you should really seek professional advice. A good auctioneer or valuer will be able to help you.

Inspecting China and Porcelain

Porcelain is one of the easiest items on which to ascertain whether or not there has been any restoration. For a start, it is transparent – if you hold a porcelain object up to a lamp or a window, you will be able to see whether or not the item is clear. If you see a blob or a dark mark, there is a strong possibility that the object has undergone some form of restoration. Next, run your fingers around the rim of the item and across

I IS FOR INK BOTTLES AND INKWELLS

The main reason that I have singled these objects out as potential investments is because the Americans love to collect them. So for all you internet dealers out there, this is an area where you can pick up items cheaply in England, put them on eBay and almost certainly grab yourself a profit.

Ink was very expensive in the 18th and 19th centuries and it was a very competitive market. In an effort to make their products more alluring, manufacturers made every effort to sell their ink in eye-catching novelties. Inkwells and bottles were fashioned from glass, salt-glazed pottery and occasionally porcelain. They came many different guises, including houses, cottages, trains, animals, clowns – some were even shaped as Napoleon. Several years ago, a square Lowestoft inkwell dating back to 1775 sold for £3,000. Obviously this is the top end of the market, as a Tiffany inkwell would also be; however, this is a great subject to collect and you could make yourself a profit.

its surface, feeling for any bumps that would also suggest work had been done on the piece.

It is somewhat harder to spot signs of restoration on china and figurines. Over time, experts have become better at restoring china, and even experienced auctioneers are tricked now and then. However, certain areas are more open to damage, and on figurines, you should focus on the hands, fingers and head.

You can also use an ultraviolet lamp to help you highlight any restoration work to china and porcelain, but these are not always available at an auction viewing. If you are buying from a reputable auction house, however, the catalogue description should tell you if the item has had any work done. If restoration work is not pointed out in the catalogue and you buy an item, only to discover at a later date that it has been tampered with, you will be able to take it back to the auction house. This applies to any item that has been catalogued incorrectly (see page 90).

Investigating Clocks

You will often find that longcase clocks, especially examples dating to the 18th century, have undergone alteration. As with furniture, you need to step back and survey a longcase clock in order to satisfy yourself that it looks in proportion. One of the most frequent changes you'll discover with a piece like this is to the base. In some cases, the clock will have been shortened, or its feet removed, as the base will have begun to rot as the floor was cleaned around it. Sometimes a broken movement inside the clock will have been replaced with new movements. Another change to look out for is a brass dial that has replaced the original painted dial; the reason for this type of substitution is that brass fixtures generally tend to be worth more money. Once again, if you are going to invest in a longcase clock you will need to take advice from the auctioneer, or research the subject yourself. You will be amazed by how much you will learn by trawling through a specialist book for an hour and studying images of other examples before you view a sale yourself.

The information above provides just a brief summary of what to look out for when buying antiques. Inspection, inspection, inspection should be a mantra when attending auctions – it is one of the most important things to remember when investing money in antiques.

Job Lots

Most auction houses conduct several types of sale. The most prominent type deals with fine art and collectables, and the secondary sales come under the banner 'Victorian and general'. The latter is where you will find job lots. These come about if an auction house has been asked to clear an entire estate. In doing so, the better items are selected for the primary sale, with any other items placed in a Victorian and general auction sale. From the auctioneer's point of view, this is a great way to get rid of everything from the estate that will sell at auction. A catalogue description of a job lot may read something like 'shelf containing collectables', along with the words 'highlights to include', and then Doulton, Beswick or whatever else is worthy of description. Auction houses place minimum values on job lots of perhaps £20 or £50, although some set these as high as £100.

If the contents of an estate includes a specialist collection – for example, eggcups, inkwells or cruet sets – these may be put together as a job lot and catalogued as such. This does not mean that the auctioneer thinks that these items are worthless; rather, the saleroom is trying to target a specialist collector who will buy the whole lot in one go. This does actually work, and it is one of the best ways to dispose of a client's contents and achieve the best price.

If you intend to bid on a job lot, the first thing you need to do is check the condition of every single item in the lot. Look for cracks, chips or any other signs of damage; only then can you ascertain what sort of price you are willing to pay for the job lot. This sort of lot is targeted at the

J IS FOR JUKEBOX

With a definite upsurge of nostalgia for the rock 'n' roll era, juke-boxes have become a prime target for collectors. However, collecting jukeboxes is not cheap and they are quite rare. Some jukeboxes are stocked with the discs that increase the item's value. Others allow you the enjoyment of building up your own collection of discs. Prices start at anything from £2,000, with some examples reaching over £10,000 – but what a fabulous and fun item to have in your collection.

Obviously, if you are going to invest in a jukebox you need to have a lot of room. They are also quite gaudy, so make sure your other half is happy about your purchase before you decide to invest.

Most of the collectable jukeboxes originate from the United States, with one name in particular springing to mind: Wurlitzer. A good example of a Wurlitzer from the 1940s could cost you well over £10,000. A lot depends on the style and design of piece; some models have flashing lights all around them and these tend to be among the priciest examples. Move forward to the 1970s, and the style and design of jukeboxes is not nearly as striking as the earlier models, but pieces from this period will still cost a couple of thousand pounds.

There are English-made jukeboxes that are collectable, including the Chantal 'Meteor'. This model was produced between 1958 and 1973 and held an incredible selection of 200 discs. Meteors now make £5,000–£7,000 at auction.

The cheapest jukeboxes date from the 1980s, and are still worth the investment, costing £500–£800.

antiques trade, and so you will be bidding against either collectors or antique dealers, or both. Don't be put off by this possible competition, however, as by now you should know your subject, know what a good price is and have a good feel for the market. The arrival of eBay (see pages 86–89) has made the competition for job lots even stiffer – just be prepared to hold your nerve for a bidding war!

J IS FOR JIGSAW PUZZLES

Jigsaw puzzles can prove to be a very cheap and enjoyable area in which to collect. Before the arrival of television they were a great form of family entertainment and were particularly prolific from the beginning of the 20th century to the 1930s.

Jigsaw puzzles were invented in 1760 by a London-based cartographer. He mounted a map on a sheet of mahogany and then cut it out into small pieces with a fine saw so that he could teach his pupils geography. The idea caught on and was soon copied by other manufacturers. The jigsaws from this early period were handmade and quite expensive to buy, but still proved popular. Common themes for the scenes depicted on these early puzzles included religion, history and mythology. Names to look out for from this period include Dean & Son, W. Peacock and J. Betts; their jigsaws are much sought after by collectors.

At the end of the 19th century, manufacturers started to paste a coloured label on the jigsaw boxes, which displayed the finished image. Some of these late-19th-century jigsaws are definitely worth collecting now. In the early 1900s techniques for making jigsaws improved and mass production began. By the 1920s jigsaws had become a veritable craze.

If you do intend to build a collection of jigsaw puzzles I suggest that you stick to a single manufacturer. Among the famous firms that produced jigsaws was Chad Valley, a Birmingham-based company, which created some incredible puzzles that depicted subjects including the Great Eastern Railway and the great vessels of the age from the Cunard and White Star shipping lines. These Chad Valley puzzles are worth looking out for; for an example from the 1920s–30s you can expect to pay £40–£60. Most boxes state how many pieces should be in a puzzle. It is not easy to stand and count each piece when buying a puzzle at an antiques fair or an auction, but it is time well spent, as to hold its value a jigsaw puzzle needs to be complete.

Another way of utilizing an early jigsaw is to complete the puzzle and frame it, as they actually look rather stunning.

Sleepers

The other thing to look out for in a job lot is the 'sleeper'. A sleeper is an item of value that has been overlooked by the auctioneer. For example, amongst a shelf of blue-and-white china there just might be an early piece of Royal Worcester; that shelf of Art Deco collectables could just contain a small piece of Clarice Cliff. This is why you need to look very hard at the contents of a job lot. Do not be afraid to dig down to the bottom of the box – you may just find a hidden gem. (For more about sleepers, see pages 100–101.)

Just Where Did These Goods Come From?

Many buyers at an auction house are inquisitive as to where the goods actually came from. Are they being sold by an estate? Or by a company which is liquidating? Or have they come from a trader? I was often asked this question as an auctioneer and in fact it is a rather delicate subject. Most auctioneers have a confidentiality policy with their clients, which includes both the buyer and the seller. However, it is a question you are free to ask and some auctioneers will give you the answer. Reading the auction catalogue highlights will also sometimes reveal this information; indeed, many auction rooms take great pleasure in announcing that they are auctioning the entire contents of a local country house, for example.

Many auctioneers also hold liquidation sales, where a company has gone bankrupt and the administrators have instructed the auction house to dispose of their assets. These are often good sales to attend, as most if not all of the items will be sold with no reserve. Other auction houses have on-site auctions, whereby the auction room goes to a country estate and sells the complete contents on behalf of the owner. Such sales are always very well attended, as most dealers like goods to be fresh to the market. Some of the goods in such sales have not been seen on the open market for hundreds of years, so you will have to expect to pay a premium. However, bargains can still be had, so don't be put off.

If you are a regular attendee at an auction house, you can guarantee that some of the lots will have been entered by the trade. Traders need to turn their stock over, so will buy in a general sale, restore the item and then re-enter it in the hope of making a profit. There is nothing wrong in this, and if you are a regular visitor to an auction house you will be able to spot the trade pieces and the restored lots.

Keeping Things in Good Condition

I cannot stress enough how important it is to keep your antiques in tip-top condition, and there is no reason for you not to do this, as it is easy to achieve. All too often I'm asked to value an antique piece of furniture, only to discover that what should be a marvellous Georgian chest of drawers has a huge gash down its side. I usually only have to check behind the piece of furniture to find the dreaded radiator that has dried the wood out and caused it to crack. Or I might be called to value a painting that should be worth £1,000, but which can only be valued at £250, as it has been kept in direct sunlight and the colours have faded badly.

There are some golden rules when it comes to preserving antiques. One of the most important is to remember that most antiques were made before the advent of central heating or radiators. Temperatures within buildings were a lot cooler, and were guided by the seasons, with little in the way of artificial heat sources or air conditioning. Winter would have been very cold, and the summer, mellow and warm. These conditions ensured that the objects that we now consider antiques lasted through the years.

Furniture

To emphasize the point I've made: you should never place furniture close

66

K IS FOR KNIFE BOXES

Knife boxes were unique to the 18th and 19th centuries. They were normally highly decorative and were very decadent in their day. Made by superior craftsmen, knife boxes are highly collectable items that come in many shapes and forms. They normally took the form of a box with a lid, which would stand on a table or sideboard and open to reveal the knife. Many examples still exist and some of the most desirable examples are decorated on the exterior and interior.

to or in front of a radiator or a heater, as this will dry out the wood and cause cracks to appear. The heat source will also cause the glue to become unstuck and the veneer will lift. You must also never keep antique furniture in the path of direct sunlight. If this proves impossible, then I suggest pulling down the blinds, or drawing the curtains when the sun is at its strongest.

Preserving antique furniture is quite simple. You need to give it a good coat of wax once every six weeks, as this will enhance the patina, or sheen. In fact, one of the charms of antiques is this natural patina, which is achieved after years of wax and polishing. Buyers favour this when selecting their antiques – they love to see 250-years' worth of grime rubbed into the beeswax. Once you have seen a piece of furniture in this condition, it becomes apparent why it is so collectable and desirable. So keep your antique furniture out of the sun, away from radiators and heaters, polish and wax frequently and finally, if you have to move your item, do so with care.

Paintings and Prints

Watercolours and prints that have been framed behind glass tend to stay in good condition. They are, however, susceptible to mildew and 'foxing', a condition that is caused when moisture in the air gets into the back of the frame and causes spots and marks that discolour the paper. To avoid foxing, it is worth taking your picture off the wall on a regular basis to check that the backing is intact. If you discover that rust has started to affect the nails on the backing paper, this is a sure sign that the painting needs urgent attention, as the rust indicates the presence of water attacking the metal. Foxing can be repaired easily by a good restorer. It is worth attending to the matter as soon as you notice it, because it can seriously affect the price of a picture.

Another rule to remember is that you must never hang a painting or a print in direct sunlight. Some Victorian watercolours are particularly susceptible to daylight, so the darker the area they are kept in, the better. To show off the true colour of a painting, place a light above it.

Oil paintings also need care and attention. Gently dust the canvas on a regular basis, using a feather duster to get rid of any dirt accumulating on the front of the painting. You also need to check the back of the canvas, as dust will also gather here.

Sometimes frames can pose a problem, as some antique paintings involve intricately carved gesso, a fine white plaster that is very fragile. Be careful when moving these types of frames, as something as small as a thumbprint can partially destroy the gesso on a gilt frame. Frames of this nature should be treated with extreme delicacy. A light sweep with a feather duster will work wonders, but use a soft toothbrush for any built-in grime. It is worth remembering that some 18th- and 19th-century gilt and gesso frames are almost as valuable as the painting mounted within them. If you have a frame of this description that needs repair, you must consult an expert – cheap restoration of a valuable frame will halve its value.

Silver

Collectors look for a crisp appearance when it comes to silver. Air tends to tarnish this metal, causing greenish-brown stains, so silver items need to be stored inside a proper glazed cabinet. As well, care should be taken when cleaning silver, as it is actually possible to over-clean the metal when trying to achieve the perfect sparkle, and this will affect the value of the piece. Time and time again, I have seen once-beautiful pieces of silver that have been polished so frequently and harshly that the hallmark has been rubbed away. Not only does this devalue the item, it also makes it harder to date. One of the best ways to clean silver is by using silver mitts; these are worn on the hand and rubbed gently over the object. This method will bring a silver piece back to its former glory. If your silver is kept in a cabinet, you only need to polish it once a month.

Antiques made from silver plate also need to be treated appropriately, as there is only a thin layer of silver covering the copper beneath it. If a piece in silver plate is over-cleaned, the copper will start to show through.

K IS FOR KODAK CAMERAS

Kodak cameras revolutionized photography. They were one of the first companies to mass-produce cameras for the general public. The early box cameras, which date to the turn of the 20th century, have become increasingly collectable. However, if you come across one of these, make sure that the squeezebox, which you'll be able to find by opening the camera, is not damaged before you buy.

Plastic and bakelite cameras arrived later in the 20th century, and these are now fast becoming collector's items in their own right. If the camera has its original packaging, the price is enhanced. Colour variations also affect value; black and brown were the most common colours, but I have seen examples in red, yellow and green.

Although there are many camera manufacturers on the market, Kodak has always been regarded as 'the people's' camera manufacturer. A few years ago the box cameras could be found at boot fairs and antiques fairs for about £5, but recently I have seen them priced at £20–£30. Bakelite and plastic cameras tend to hold their price at £20–£50. Condition is always important, and scratching to the lens is one of the first things you should look out for.

If you intend to start collecting silver, you should always ensure that the hallmark is clear and has not been rubbed away. When collecting silver plate, do your research so that you can tell if an item has been re-plated. Although this is an acceptable method of restoration, it still affects price, and items that have been re-plated should be cheaper to buy.

Pottery and Porcelain

Items made from china and porcelain should also be kept in cabinets, to stop layers of dust from building up. In my opinion, gentle cleaning with a light feather duster is the only way to clean 18th- and 19th-century century china and porcelain. If you submerge these items in warm, soapy water they will re-emerge as nice, shiny pieces, but this sort of cleaning will also damage the delicate hand-painting on the surface of the china, causing it to fade and ultimately disappear. I cannot stress enough that you need to clean antique pottery and porcelain with the utmost of care. On too many occasions I have seen porcelain and china items that should display gilded borders or highlights, yet these have completely disappeared as a result of heavy-handed cleaning.

K IS FOR KITCHENWARE

Kitchenware provides huge scope for would-be collectors. Many items that fall under this label are relatively cheap, and there are so many unusual and quirky items to discover – including storage jars, enamel breadbins, kitchen gadgets, mincers, slicers and herb cutters – that collecting kitchen implements is enormously enjoyable. Also called 'kitchenalia', prices for items in this category start at a few pounds and can rise to several hundred.

Among the most interesting items to collect are moulds for jelly and other foodstuffs. Eating habits became very elaborate in Victorian times, and diners sat through many courses. Food thus needed to be decorative as well as filling, and ornamental moulds formed a favourite Victorian centrepiece: the more decorative the food looked, the more appetizing it appeared. Rumour has it that Apsley House, the home of the Duke of Wellington, was home to over 500 different types of moulds to hold jelly, ice cream, mousse and other foods. Early moulds were usually ceramic or metal, but from the late 19th century, pressed glass was also used to fashion them. Moulds are a fascinating area of collectables, as they come in all shapes and sizes, some of the most popular being animals. The value depends on the medium, shape, condition and size. The more elaborate the design, the higher the price will be. Expect to pay anything between £10–£200.

When purchasing kitchenware items, it is often wise to buy those that you can use in your own kitchen. I know one individual who has been collecting antique pans and jelly moulds for the past 30 years. It always amazes me how well the food cooks – the taste seems to be enhanced by these aged implements. Among this individual's collection is a superb fruit-shaped blancmange mould and a marvellous

A Final Word About Keeping Antiques in Good Condition

It is imperative that you look after your antiques properly, and clean them appropriately. If you are unsure about the best way to clean a particular item, approach an expert or a friendly dealer for advice. There are also many books available on how to clean and care for your antiques.

1930s hand-whisk. The whole kitchen is a shrine to antique kitchenware, all of which is used on a regular basis.

Coffee grinders are another excellent item to collect, and many different examples were produced from the late 19th to early 20th century. Grinders from the first quarter of the 19th century are some of the most desirable for collectors. Items from this period had brass or copper bowls to collect the ground coffee; when buying a grinder from this period, you need to check that this area is in good condition, as it is normally the weakest part of the object. You can find some very well-designed coffee grinders from the early 20th century, which come in many unusual shapes and are easily affordable; the price range is generally £30–£80.

Enamelware is another area of kitchenalia that is worth collecting. Enamelled metal was first mass-produced in the late 19th century, and is still produced today. Many antique enamel items, including breadbins, storage jars and saucepans, have survived decades. Even pieces that show signs of wear and tear are collectable. An object that bears the name of the product it contains is more desirable than a plain item. Look out for items with unusual labels, for example, 'breadcrumbs', 'raisins', 'currants', 'sultanas' or 'baking soda'. Many enamel items can still be found at boot fairs, collectors' fairs and even charity shops. One thing to watch out for: before 1930 the interior of these enamel storage jars was white, but after this date the interior was the same colour as the exterior

One period of kitchenware that is definitely worth seeking out is the 1950s. Items from this period, including food mixers, soda makers, kettles, toasters and even fridges, have that distinctive 'retro' look that has inspired many a modern kitchen implement.

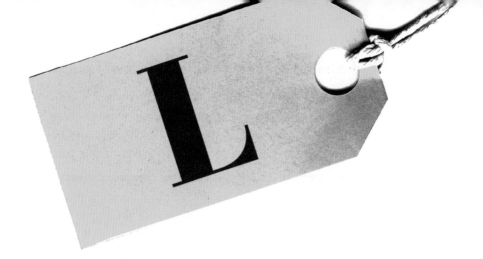

Learning the Hard Way

This section really encapsulates what antiques and collecting are all about. So many mistakes are made through lack of knowledge, and I cannot emphasize strongly enough how important it is to know your product before you buy. One of the hardest jobs an auctioneer has is to tell a client that the item he or she has paid £300 for is only worth £150, because, for example, they have failed to notice that the porcelain vase just purchased has a hairline crack on it, or the legs of the chair they've bought have been replaced, or the leather-tooled surface of a writing desk is modern, not of the period.

Knowing what you're buying comes with experience, and once again, this can only be achieved through many hours of reading, researching and viewing. Imagine, for instance, that you are keen on objects from the Art Deco period. Let's assume that you have become friendly with a few dealers that specialize in the period – you will be amazed at how much knowledge they will share with you if you show a keen and friendly interest. Don't forget that you are also a potential buyer in their eyes, and that they want to sell their wares to you.

It should also be enjoyable to collect antiques. When you start to build a collection, remember that you can always upgrade your items and start to invest more money as your confidence and knowledge of the subject grows. A good phrase to lodge in your memory is the old adage: look, listen and learn.

If you do make a mistake, the worse thing you can do is to dwell on it. Don't turn into the fisherman who's always talking about the 'one that got away'. If you have a positive attitude, then you will always have another chance in the antiques game.

Local Salerooms

Local salerooms are very important to collectors, especially if you intend to become a trader. By 'local' I mean any saleroom that is within about 20 miles of where you live, and that you are able to attend regularly. Having a local saleroom is like having a local pub: you will get to know the auctioneers, cashier and the porters.

It is particularly good to get to know the porters at your local sale-room, as they are one of its most important assets. These individuals do all the hard work, clearing houses and packing up items to take to the auction room, and moving the furniture about in the saleroom. Porters also make sure the antiques look good when put on view. Most importantly, the porters know where the goods have come from, and indeed, how 'honest' they are. If you want to get to know your local porters, it's worth tipping them when they help you. Up until the 1980s, many porters who worked in auction rooms were totally reliant on tips provided by clients. As a rough guide, a tip should be between £2–£10, and should be given to the porter when he or she helps you to your car with the goods. Some porters will also execute your bids for you if you are unable to attend the sale.

Fresh lots to a local saleroom tend to attract a lot of attention from traders, as they know that these lots have come from a local estate clearance, and have not been in a shop; or perhaps they have come from a trader who has restored them. Most auction rooms will take in trade items, and it is important that you get to know what a trade lot looks like, as it will save you from buying a lot that may have been sitting in an antiques shop for the past six months. There is absolutely nothing wrong in buying a trade lot, as long as the price is right and it suits your requirements. Several traders I know like to turn their stock around regularly, and if a piece has remained in their shop for too long and they can't get a good retail price for it, many are happy to sell the lot for a similar price to what they initially paid for it. Again, this is a good example of why you should get to know the porters at your local auction room, as they can guide you through the lots and tell you about the provenance of the items for sale.

L IS FOR LIBERTY

Liberty is the upmarket store based on Regent Street in London and synonymous with the top end of the antiques and collectables market. In the early 20th century, Liberty almost single-handedly introduced the Art Nouveau and Arts & Crafts movements to the English elite.

A department on the top floor of the building has dealt in Art Nouveau and Arts & Crafts goods for the past 100 years. Dealing primarily in furniture, Liberty also introduced things like Tudric Pewter, which was produced by Archibald Knox and many other top designers of the period. Liberty's buyers scoured the country to source goods for the store. Many of the items that retailed through the store carry the Liberty & Co mark.

When trying to determine whether an item of Art Nouveau furniture is Liberty or not, look closely at the piece. If it has a very strong Art Nouveau design to it, particularly on the brass or copper handles, take one of the handles off. A Liberty item will have the mark L & C impressed on it, which stands for Liberty & Co. Many an astute dealer has made a good profit by knowing this trade secret.

Throughout the 20th century Liberty continued to be innovative and inspirational, introducing new names to the antiques and collectables world. Among Liberty's major successes were Moorcroft in the 1900s and Troika in the 1960s. A visit to the store today will be a pleasant surprise for any budding collector.

You also need to have the correct attitude towards the auctioneer at your local saleroom, as he or she is in charge of the room and actually conducts the sales there. It is important that you treat him or her with due respect. Once you are on friendly terms with the auctioneer, he or she will remember which lots you have bid on in the past, and will likely inform you when he or she hears that a lot you might be interested in is coming up.

When you first attend a local saleroom, it might seem a little bit like a private members club. At the back of the saleroom, a group of furniture dealers might be huddled; seated opposite will be a group of general dealers, and sitting in the seats below the auctioneer will be the collec-

L IS FOR LONGCASE CLOCKS

A very wise investment over the last few decades has been the longcase, or grandfather, clock. This description covers two different types of clock. The first is a 30-hour clock, normally called a country clock, which has a single weight behind the door. The second is an 8-day clock, which has two weights behind the door – these are the most desirable examples to look out for. Longcase clocks vary tremendously, spanning from fine-quality examples made by master craftsmen to country clocks made by less experienced horologists. The clocks that make the most money are those that were made in London, and have fine walnut cases. To demonstrate how sound an investment some antiques can be, a clock matching this description could have been bought for £2,000–£3,000 in the 1980s. Today it would now cost you at least £12,000–£15,000. A 30-hour clock snapped up for as little as £100–£150 at the same time would now cost you at least ten times as much – up to £3,000. Longcase clocks are a good example of how things go in and out of fashion, as many of these items found their way onto scrap heaps in the 1960s and early 1970s, when they were considered ugly.

tors and locals. Many of these individuals will sit through the entire auction. This atmosphere may be quite daunting on your first visit, but once you become accustomed to it, you will become confident in your bidding. Once you have attended your local saleroom a couple of times, rest assured that you will get to know the regulars. Auction rooms tend to be friendly places, with plenty of tea, coffee and sandwiches available!

Marketing and Media

These are two very important matters to consider if you intend to become an antiques dealer, whether you want to enter the profession in a part-time or full-time capacity. Like any business, the way in which you market and present yourself is very important. Equally, the manner in which you sell your items, and the way they are perceived by the buying public, are crucial to your success. Even if you start off with a small stall at an antiques fair and then progress to an antiques shop, you will need to bear this in mind.

Setting Up a Stall

I have been to many antiques fairs where I have walked straight past some stalls because they look as if they are peddling junk: there is nothing to catch your immediate attention, and everything on the stall is a jumbled mess, with not a price tag in sight. However, a stall with decorative shelving, a smartly dressed attendant and spotlights highlighting the better pieces for sale is likely to attract positive attention. If you set up your stall in this latter fashion, you will find that you will immediately attract buyers who will not hesitate to stop and look at your stall.

It is also well worth remembering that antiques fairs tend to attract regular visitors, and so it is important to vary the look of your stall and to change your stock regularly. It is also worth placing business cards on your stand, as these indicate that you are a serious dealer. Furthermore, many private sellers visit antiques fairs, and they may have something that they want to sell to you. This is a good way of acquiring fresh stock without having to search for it.

Showing Off your Shop

If you have an antiques shop, it is important that the window, which is really your showcase, is changed frequently. There is nothing worse than walking past an antiques shop every day and seeing exactly the same thing in the window for months on end. To attract passing trade, you

M IS FOR MIDWINTER

Founded in 1910, the Midwinter ceramics company quickly developed from a small family business into one of the larger potteries in Stoke-on-Trent, but it was not until after the Second World War, when Roy Midwinter, the son of the founder, took over as design director, that the company really took off. He was influenced by potteries on the American West Coast, and when his 'Stylecraft' shape was launched in 1953, it broke the mould for traditional British ceramics. The 'Fashion' shape of 1955 was even more extreme. Midwinter's excellent in-house designers, including Jesse Tate, Hugh Casson and Terence Conran, gave the factory a big lead over its competitors.

There are particular items you should look for from the 1950s. The zebra-like 'Zambezi' pattern by Jesse Tate is very collectable, as are the red 'Domino' and the 'Festival' patterns. When collecting Midwinter, you need to look at the shape and design and assess whether or not it epitomizes the 1950s – if it does, then it will be collectable. I'm sure that these items will go up in value, and you can still find them cheaply in charity shops and at boot fairs.

In the 1960s, Midwinter stayed one step ahead of its competitors when it launched David Queensbury's 'Fine' shape in 1962. Patterns from this period are now beginning to become popular with 1960s collectors. They are still relatively cheap to buy, but I think that they will go up in price in the not too distant future.

M IS FOR MOORCROFT

Moorcroft pottery is one of a blue chip group of collectables that is unlikely to ever go out of fashion. Moorcroft formed as a design studio under the umbrella of a large English ceramics company called Macintyre and Co. The company produced a vast range of distinctive items, including decorative vases, tableware, commemorative items and table lamps.

The company's first successful range, designed by William Moorcroft, was called Florian and was produced from 1898–1906. These items are among the most desirable and collectable Moorcroft ceramics. The range was so successful that it was financed by the upmarket London department store Liberty. Florian displayed an instantly recognizable blend of Art Nouveau and the decorative traditions of William Morris and the Arts and Crafts movement. There are many different Florian patterns to look out for, many based on English flowers, such as poppies, tulips, forget-me-nots, daisies and roses. Other patterns that are highly prized by Moorcroft collectors are those featuring peacock feathers, butterflies and fish. You can expect to pay anywhere from £300–£5,000 for a Florian piece, with some rare examples of the range selling for over £10,000.

Later Florian pieces tend to be more Art Nouveau in style, with designs featuring highly stylized flowers. Colourways moved on to include green and gold, and the somewhat more traditional English rose garland design on a white background.

should aim to change your window display every two weeks. I cannot stress enough that the way in which you arrange the shop's window is of the utmost importance. If you put your better items on show, then you will attract people into your shop to look at the other pieces that you have for sale. Good staff are also an important asset for a retail unit, as your clients need to be able to approach a friendly face and discuss any items in which they are interested.

Media Coverage

We are all aware of the power of the media and the importance of media coverage. Media and publicity can certainly be useful tools if you set up

Other extremely popular patterns include the Moorcroft land-scapes, such as Hazeldene. Each of these vases has a characteristic design of trees in a rolling landscape, with the tree height varying to suit the shape and size of the vase. The Hazeldene range was produced in blue and green, and dates from 1902–14. Another pattern that is highly prized is called Claremont. This is easily distinguished, as each item is decorated with toadstools.

In 1913, Moorcroft started to produce one of its most famous designs: pomegranate. This was produced in many variations, from table clocks, candlesticks and pin-trays to vases of all shapes and sizes. The range was an instant hit, and it is still enormously popular with collectors. One thing that is worth noting is that if an item has open pomegranates on it, it will be more valuable and collectable than an item displaying closed pomegranates. The range is still produced today.

Moorcroft ceramics have definitely stood the test of time; there are many books written on the subject, and many major collectors. The company continues to produce limited-edition items that are highly prized by contemporary collectors. If you are looking to buy Moorcroft, you need to examine each piece carefully, as some vases were decorated more skilfully than others. A degree of restoration is acceptable with Moorcroft ceramics, as some items were extremely fragile. Expect to pay about 50 percent less for a restored item.

in the antiques business. If you decide to take out advertising space in a local newspaper, it is always worth approaching the advertising department to suggest they run an editorial alongside your advertisement. When placing an advertisement, you will need to think about the products you are selling and buying. For example, rather than waste an advertisement by just stating what you sell, it is also worth saying, 'we buy similar items', as this is a great way to source further items for your shop.

Making A Profit

Pricing and profitability are just as important as marketing. It is fundamental that you keep a good set of books – you will need to do this for the purposes of income tax and VAT anyway. With proper records, you will be able to tell at a glance whether you have made a profit or loss at the end of every week. It is very important that you keep your eye on this: always remember that you are not in the business to lose money, but to make it.

Of course, when you set up a business you are going to have overhead costs that you will need to calculate before you consider your profits. For example, you may open a shop with a rent of £5,000 a year, which amounts to about £100 a week. Then there may be business rates of about £40 a week, and other costs such as electricity, telephone, insurance and heating, which could add another £40 a week to your outlay. This already amounts to costs of £180 a week. You might also need an advertising budget of £1,000 per year, or about £20 per week. On top of this you will need to factor in wages of about £200 per person per week. If you are working alone, it is a false economy not to pay yourself a regular wage. All this adds up to a total of £400 a week, which means that this is what you have to aim to make in profit every week. It's not going to be easy unless you know your market

You may decide to aim for a 100 percent profit margin for every item sold. Thus an item that was bought for a total cost of £100 will need to sell for £200. You should bear in mind that you will also need to replace this item. Owning a shop is a major commitment, and is definitely not the first rung of the ladder when it comes to antiques dealing. However, if you are brave enough to give it a try, I wish you good luck.

A cheaper alternative – and one that is favoured by many dealers – is to rent a stall in an antiques market (see also pages 35 and 38). Rental prices generally range from £20 per day to about £200 per week, depending on the location and size of the unit you rent. The benefit of renting such a stall is that the rent typically covers most overheads, such as electricity and water.

Managing Clients

Once you have established your antique shop, stall or antiques fair you will need to maintain a profitable business. Managing your clients effectively, whether buyers or sellers, is an important part of this process. My advice is to build yourself a client database. Many people walk into antique shops or visit antiques fairs looking for specific items. By maintaining a friendly approach to your customers you will be able to estab-

ABOVE: The Bargain Hunt *experts during the filming of the 'Champion Experts Special'. Left to right: Philip Serrell, David Barby, David 'The Duke' Dickinson, James Braxton, MH.* **BELOW:** *Victorian photograph albums in good condition are always worth looking out for, especially if dated and annotated.*

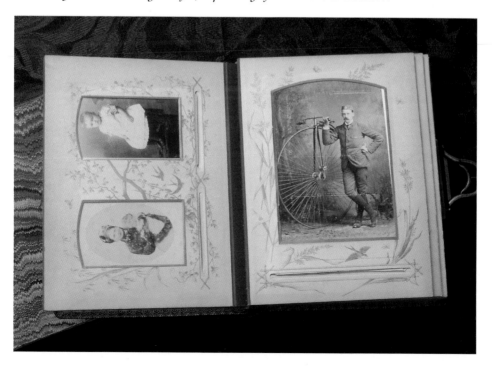

PLATE 9

ABOVE: *A selection of 18th- and 19th-century tea-caddies and tobacco boxes.*
BELOW LEFT: *Always make sure that the quality of the interior matches that of the exterior.* BELOW RIGHT: *A good example of an 18th-century bracket clock.*
OPPOSITE: *With longcase clocks always check that they are not a 'marriage' of different parts; the movements and hoods are often replaced, for example.*

PLATE 10

ABOVE: *With so many antique and secondhand shops around, it is always worth popping in just in case there's a bargain to be had!*

LEFT: *Objects from the 1940s, 50s and 60s are now very collectable, with ceramics and unusual designs of table very much in demand.*

PLATE 12

ABOVE: *Quirky objects, like this stuffed lovebird in an attractive cage, can often be picked up for a decent price and then resold later for a profit, if you choose the right sale.*

ABOVE RIGHT: *Representations of famous figures such as Napoleon will usually attract a buyer at a sale.*

RIGHT: *Coloured glass vases from the 1960s are really popular now and the best examples are becoming hard to find.*

PLATE 13

ABOVE: Costume jewellery will always command a higher price if it is in its original box, as here. ***ABOVE RIGHT:*** Always remember that you must display well to sell well! ***BELOW AND OPPOSITE:*** Vintage clothing is all the rage at the moment, but it is wise to try and anticipate the next fad or fashion and buy accordingly.

PLATE 14

ABOVE: Cold and early? Wrap up warm to bag that early bargain – it's usually worth it.

BELOW: Unframed pictures and prints should be stored away from direct sunlight at all times.

PLATE 16

lish who they are, what field they collect in and what they are looking for. Although they might not be in your shop or at your stall at any particular moment in time, there is nothing to stop you building a list of clients who are on a quest for specific items. This way you can enhance both your profitability and your turnover by having ready-made clients for items which may come your way.

Not all collectors have time on their hands to attend every single sale, and once you are a full-time antiques dealer attending as many auctions as you can, you will be amazed at how many times you will see items for which you have clients lined up. On viewing day at a sale you can check over the item and report back to the collector that you might have a particular lot coming your way in which he/she might be interested. You could even negotiate the price there and then, which makes life a lot simpler when you go to the auction to try and secure the lot. Say, for example, that the auction guide price is £150–200 but your particular collector is prepared to offer you £300. Clearly this means that there is a profit to be had! Over the months and years you will build up expertise about items you can buy for clients and make a profit from. You will also be amazed at the knowledge you will gain from these individual collectors, who often have a far superior knowledge of their specialist field.

M IS FOR MINIATURES

The best known of all miniature pieces is perhaps the furniture used in dolls' houses, for which the Victorian period spawned an endless supply of good quality furnishings, right down to wallpaper, legs of mutton, tiny lamps and babies' prams.

In the late eighties I was intrigued by a specialist sale of miniature items held by one of the top auction houses. Only when I started viewing and handling the objects did I realise their quality, particularly a William and Mary-style oyster-veneered and cross-banded chest of tiny proportions (only 7 inches tall). I was amazed to see it sell for over £2,000 against an estimate of £300–400.

What makes this kind of furniture so collectable is the fact that such pieces are the work of trainee craftsmen and apprentices, who would have had to produce this type of high-quality work before becoming true cabinet-makers.

Never Bid On These

Never be tempted to bid on a lot if you are uncertain about any aspect of it, as it can and will cost you money. There is a saying in the antiques trade, 'a little knowledge is a dangerous thing'. And when it comes to uncertainty in the auction room this definitely applies. If you have any doubt in your mind about a lot you intend to bid on, then I would advise you not to bid on it, as nine times out of ten your gut instinct is going to be correct. If the sumptuous oil painting that initially attracted your attention gives you a bad feeling on closer inspection, then walk away from it and don't be tempted to bid. You may spot a piece of furniture that would fit perfectly into a snug area at home, but you examine it to find signs of woodworm that may still be active – don't buy it, it may be untreatable. Or maybe a piece of china catches your eye, but when you give it the once over, something about it just doesn't feel right – don't be swayed. All these scenarios indicate that instinct is kicking in and telling you not to bid. However inexperienced you are, steer clear of items that make you feel like this, and do not be gripped by auction fever and get carried away (see pages 132–133). The object in question might well be something you really wanted for your collection, but, as with all antiques, you can guarantee that another example, which doesn't give you a negative vibe, will come up at some point in the future. Unless an item is utterly unique, it is a sure thing that you will come across another example.

As with everything in antiques, there are a few exceptions to this rule, but the decision is always yours to make and you must never be persuaded to buy something you are not sure about. Imagine, for example, that you are at an auction and a 10-inch-tall Clarice Cliff vase with a geometric design that would normally have an estimate of £1,500–£2,000 has been estimated at £400–£600. The catalogue listed the item as having been restored, so is it still worth buying? In this case I would think so, as there are unique or rare pieces like this on the market, and its very desirability is the reason it was restored in the first place. As with any bid, you need to use your experience and understanding of the area in which you're bidding to decide whether the item is worthy of your cash outlay.

Reproductions

As you trawl around auction rooms and antiques fairs, you will see many stalls selling reproduction antiques. Sometimes these are also called 'new' antiques. The question is, are they worth collecting? Collecting modern-day antiques is not all about profit, but having the potential to see a profit certainly helps. Many companies have reproduced earlier antiques in the hope that those who cannot afford the originals will be tempted to start collecting. For example, Wedgwood produced various Clarice Cliff items. These have proved a great success, with their market value now considerably higher than their original purchase price.

Deciding what to collect is down to individual choice and the amount you have available to invest. Each individual collector should bear in mind the following facts. A reproduction means exactly what it says; the item could be reproduced up to 500,000 times, so the chances of making a profit on this sort of investment are slim. But if something takes your fancy then there is nothing wrong in investing your cash in items you like. Many reproductions come from the Far East and are normally quite crudely made, but they do bear a resemblance to the original antique. However, once you have seen the original there is no doubt in my mind that you will then be able to spot a reproduction. Investment value for this type of object is nil.

Things to keep an eye out for are at the better end of the market, such as the factories of Doulton, Wedgwood and Coalport, which have been producing high quality goods for many years. Although the items they are producing are considered modern, within a few years they will become collectable and show a return on your money. Like all antiques

N IS FOR NEW ANTIQUES

One individual who has made a huge impact on the 'new antiques' front is Lorna Bailey. Born in 1978, she hails from Newcastle-under-Lyme and is armed with degrees in design from Stoke-on-Trent College of Art, a seat of learning that some claim to be the successor to Burslem School of Art, which is where Lorna Bailey's predecessors, namely Clarice Cliff, Susie Cooper, Charlotte Rhead and Frederick Rhead all studied. They all inspired Lorna, who creates ceramics with such striking designs that she is often referred to as the next Clarice Cliff. (While she is flattered by this accolade, Bailey prefers to be judged upon her own merits.)

Bailey was brought up around antiques, and was a collector of Wade's Whimsies as a child, moving on to collect Art Deco Ceramics, including pieces by Cliff and Cooper. These inspired her love of bold colours and unusual shapes. During the time when she was a student at Stoke, a major pottery factory, Wood & Sons, went into liquidation and its assets were put up for sale. Lorna's father, Lionel, purchased a large amount of the company's assets and took over a nearby factory. Initially, they produced hand-painted wares, including Toby jugs and decorated ceramics.

Lorna spent much of her free time working for the business, painting and experimenting with her works. By 1998 sales of her work had increased to the point that she had two staff hand-painting ceramics for her and producing exclusive designs bearing her name. Some of these early examples are highly sought after. Most of Lorna Bailey's designs are limited editions. One particular example of her popularity was illustrated in 1998 when *Collect It* magazine asked her to produce an item called the 'Astro' sugar sifter. A limited edition of 250 was produced, coinciding with the magazine's next issue. It sold out immediately, inspiring the magazine to commission another 250 for their next issue. This edition sold out before the magazines reached the newsagents. The demand for her work was such that a collectors' club was formed, which is still in operation today. Her works are certainly stunning and have a distinctive, stylized Art Deco feel to them. Lorna Bailey is definitely a designer to keep your eye on, and her works are an excellent example of 'new' antiques.

you intend to invest in, the quality of the item is absolutely central. If you are thinking of buying a figurine, for example, then check the quality of the face, hands and feet. Good quality items will always shine through when it comes to re-sale.

Furniture and furnishings are on many people's shopping lists when they move home, but deciding what to buy for your new loft apartment, house or cottage can be one of the hardest decisions. I would suggest you think ahead, but remember that at some stage you might want to change your décor. Buying furniture from a retail unit can be like buying a brand new car: once out of the showroom, the price drops by half. This really cannot be avoided unless you are wise enough to go to an auction sale, at which you will be able to buy modern items of furniture at a fraction of the retail cost. However, not everyone can make time to attend auction sales, and retail units do have a good selection of modern furniture, ranging from stylized and modern designs right through to traditional country oak. Always remember that a retail unit will always be prepared to haggle, and so never be afraid to ask for that extra discount.

Online Auctions

Are online auctions going to take the place of the traditional auction room? I don't think so, although they are gaining a significant foothold in the market for antiques and collectables. The primary difference is that in an auction house, buyers and sellers alike get to meet each other. They get to touch and see the goods they are purchasing, which is extremely important when buying antiques. And of course, it is hard to beat the atmosphere in an auction room, and the buzz of bidding for a lot in person – it all adds to the excitement of buying antiques.

The King of Online Marketplaces: eBay

The major online auction website, eBay, has been a phenomenon. Founded in the United States in 1995, it has created a huge market for the sale of all types of goods, including antiques. It has a global presence and on any given day there are millions of items listed on the site, covering such diverse categories as antiques, toys, books, computers, sport, photographs, electronics – you name it and I guarantee you will find it on eBay. The site was launched in Britain in 1999, but it has already established itself as the largest online marketplace in the country. By February 2005 eBay had hit the 10-million-user milestone – that's a lot of potential buyers viewing your lots. It really is a great way to buy or sell anything – even a private jet was sold on eBay, albeit for a whopping US$4.6 million dollars. This method of trading has had some effect on auction rooms, as most auctioneers will agree.

One of the greatest things about eBay is that the world of collectables and collecting is quite literally at your fingertips. Joining eBay is really very simple. When you open the homepage, you are given full instructions on how to register, providing your name and address; country of residence; phone number; date of birth; and, most importantly, your email address. Once you have entered your details, you are given a code, or a user name, which enables you to bid and sell on the website.

Finding items on eBay is a piece of cake. The site itself has been structured to meet public demand, and is one of the most frequently used sites on the internet. You simply type in the name or a description of the item you are looking for – whether it's an ashtray or an airplane – and click on the search engine – you'll be amazed at how many items will come up on screen. Each item on the list will be accompanied by an image and a brief description. Once you click on an item, a page will open providing a fuller description that will explain all you need to know about the item on offer. It will tell you what the current bid is; how long you have left to bid; the time at which the item was posted on the site; the number of bids the object has received; and where the item is located. You will also be provided with a postage cost – you need to look closely at this, as it can be quite expensive, particularly if the item is bulky or if it is in another country. If you decide that the item is for you, you need to place your bid in the bid column. You will then be asked to confirm your bid – once this has been done, you cannot retract it. The item is monitored so that every time you open your eBay account, you are updated on the status of your lot – you will be told if you have been outbid. Once the time period that the seller has selected is up, you will be informed whether or not you have been successful in your purchase.

Another great thing about eBay is that you can allocate a favourite search. For example, if you are looking for something in particular, you can just type the item in, add it to your favourite searches and eBay will e-mail you if anything comes up on the site that might be of interest to you. However, it's worth being cautious about this, as I made the mistake of adding 20 items to my list of favourites, so that most days I get 20 emails from eBay!

Paying for the goods you buy on eBay is very simple. Most sellers accept 'Paypal', which is an online banking system that allows you to register your credit details (they are, of course, confidential). Once you have registered, any transaction that you conduct on the site can be filtered through the Paypal system. Some eBay sellers also accept cheques or other forms of payment, but Paypal tends to be the most popular system of payment.

Once you have paid for your goods, you will normally receive them within five to seven days. If you encounter any problems, eBay has a helpline that you can contact. It is worth checking the seller's information before you bid, as this will tell you how many items they have sold previously on the website and how they are rated by bidders – positive, neutral or negative. The better the rating, the more positive the feedback has been. It is always worth looking out for eBay traders that have received positive feedback, as they tend to be regular sellers and buyers.

Selling on eBay

The cost of selling on eBay is relatively cheap, and there is no charge for buyers – except delivery, which can be pricey, depending on where the item you're buying is located. You can list your items for a three-, seven- or ten-day period, at the end of which your items will be sold to the highest bidder, as they would in any auction room. You can also include a photograph, which will help with the sale of your items. To do this you need a digital camera, but it is very easy to download the photos on to the site. It has to be said that eBay makes auctioning very easy.

Selling goods on eBay is also very simple once you have opened your account. Click on the 'sell' button and you will be given complete instructions. You will be given the option of writing a description for your item, adding a picture and setting your price. The company does charge a fee for selling your items, and the price structure is very competitive when compared with auction houses. The website also charges a small listing fee for each item you place on it.

If you decide to put a reserve on your item, you will be charged a fee if the lot does not sell. Thus before you place your items on eBay, it is advisable to find out what the items are actually worth. One way to avoid paying this fee is to put a starting price on the lot rather than a reserve price. If, for instance, you decide to put a £100 reserve on your item, it will cost you about £5, whether the lot sells or not. If, however, you put a £100 starting price on the item, you will only have to pay the listing fees. This is worth bearing in mind, as it can save you money. Another thing to consider if you decide to sell on eBay is how much the postage will cost. Most items sold on the site tend to be small items, which can be easily packed and sent through the post. Larger items need to be picked up by a carrier or collected by the prospective purchaser.

The description you provide for your item is very important for prospective buyers. The more detailed, accurate and clear the description is, the easier it will be to sell the item. Remember to measure the lots you are selling, and if the item you sell has any maker's marks, it is worth taking a photograph of them. Once you have posted the item on eBay, you will be sent notification confirming that the lot has been listed. The website also provides a counter for sellers, so that every time you view your lot, you will see how many other people have viewed your item. You will also be able to see how many people are watching your item – this is quite important, as this means that there are buyers interested in how much your lot is selling for.

As with all online auctions, there is normally a frenzy of bidding towards the end of the listing period. I recommend the ten-day listing, as this means you can cover two weekends. A ten-day listing usually attracts more interested bidders.

Sitting in the comfort of your own home, you can still get some of the excitement of an auction room. When an item comes to the end of its listing period, it is always good fun to watch the bidding, as, with any luck, the price will continuously rise, and, like all auctions, it really does depend on who really wants the item on the day. Many people who bid on eBay leave their bidding until the last 20 minutes of the listing period. Some bidders also leave a covering bid in the hope that no one else has noticed the item.

One useful tip when participating in online auctions is to search for mis-spelt or incorrectly dated items. It is quite amazing how many people can't spell Worcester or Troika, or think that a piece of Poole pottery originates in the 1930s, when it is actually from 1900. Of course, you really have got to know your stuff to do this, but it is certainly worth typing in a few incorrect spellings to see if you can find a bargain.

You should not be daunted by the prospect of joining eBay, as it is actually one of the easiest ways to deal in antiques and experience the auction process. It can also be very profitable, and is always great fun. You can do your Christmas shopping on eBay, or build a collection.

Such is the phenomenon of eBay that there are now books written solely on this subject. I'm sure that over the years the site will grow and grow, along with the internet. Nevertheless, many individuals, myself included, still agree that the best way to buy and sell antiques is in an auction room. But for those who cannot attend sales in person, an online auction is a great place to start on the path to becoming an antiques dealer or collector.

The Purchaser's Rights

As with any business transaction, purchasers in an auction room have legal rights. When buying at a saleroom, these rights normally come down to how an item has been described in the catalogue.

Imagine that you visit an auction house, where you decide to bid on Lot 64, the description for which reads 'matching set of six Victorian dining chairs, estimate £600–£900'. You successfully purchase the set for £800, but when you show them to your local antiques dealer he or she informs you that the set of chairs is actually a copy that dates to the 1950s. In a situation like this you have every legal right to return these chairs to the auction room and demand your money back, as the items were incorrectly catalogued by the auction room.

If, however, the chairs were described as a 'set of six Victorian *style* dining chairs, estimate £600–£900', and you paid £800, you would have no cause for redress. The catalogue description clearly states that these are in the 'style' of Victorian chairs, which informs you that they are reproductions. This is why you need to carefully read and understand the descriptions in an auction catalogue.

As another example, if you were to purchase an item that is catalogued as an 18-carat-gold Victorian period brooch, but on further inspection you discover that it is only 9-carat gold, you are again perfectly entitled to return the item to the auction house and demand your money back.

P IS FOR PLAYING CARDS

Playing cards are a fascinating collector's item, with an even more fascinating history. If you have the patience to hunt down rare cards, you will find that they are by no means expensive.

Early playing cards, dating from about 1712–1862, are very easy to date by looking at the ace of spades. During this period, excise tax was levied on each pack, and one card in every pack was stamped with a distinctive mark showing that duty had been paid. The ace of spades was selected to indicate this. Wrappers were also sealed and stamped. Of course, this created an illicit trade in bogus aces, which grew to such heights that by 1756 it was made a crime to counterfeit or forge any duty aces. I discovered that an engraver was actually executed in 1762 for merely possessing a copper plate engraved with duty aces.

Because of the boom in illegal trade, the commissioners tried to limit the number of playing card manufacturers, confining their trade to the cities of London, Westminster and Dublin. They issued licences, which cost £500 and acted as security against forgery. The aces themselves were printed by the commissioners at Somerset House in London, which is where the card manufacturers had to go to pay duty on the aces they required.

Duty on playing cards lasted till 1862, when it cost 3d. In fact, some playing cards carried the inscription 'duty 3d when used in Great Britain & Ireland' up until the early 20th century.

If you do come across some early playing cards, you might wonder how they were actually used. They had rough surfaces that were easily soiled, and had plain backs. It was not until 1862 that figureheads were added to playing cards; letters for the royal characters appeared from 1884, rounded corners from 1862 and double-headed cards from 1867. Playing cards from the 1920s–1950s are also collectable. As with all collectables, the playing cards you collect really need to epitomize the period in which they were created. Like all antiques, I sometimes think that these items should be used and enjoyed, but if they are in their cellophane wrappers then they shouldn't be opened. However, if they have been used before, they will provide a great conversation piece while playing whist or bridge.

Most auction houses will accept their mistakes, and will pay you back immediately, as they tend to hold clients' money for at least 28 days until all the goods are cleared from the saleroom. I must state, though, that it is becoming a rarity for things to be catalogued incorrectly, particularly at fine art sales, as most auctioneers and valuers offer excellent detailed

P IS FOR POOLE POTTERY

Being a big fan of the Dorset town of Poole, and an even bigger fan of the pottery produced there, I could not omit to tell you about one of my favourite companies.

Poole pottery was established in 1873, and still continues to trade today. From 1873 until 1920, the company produced some fine ceramics, stoneware and tiles. For me, the company landed on the map in the 1921, with the formation of Carter, Stabler & Adams, a partnership that took over the factory that year. Collectors love items from this period, although some of the earlier designs from the late 19th century to 1920 are also highly collectable. Among my favourite pieces are Truda Carter's geometric and abstract floral designs. They are absolutely stunning works, commanding high prices in auction rooms. Other artists working for Poole in this period, for example Ruth Pavely and Anne Hatchard, have also become very collectable.

The company went from strength to strength in the 1920s and the 1930s, producing objects in all shapes and sizes. One particular range that was ahead of its time was called 'Streamline'. Produced in the 1935 and designed by John Adams, this was a simple, two-tone range in brown and cream, green and cream or pink and grey. There was a vast selection of objects in the range, including 'Breakfast in Bed' sets, 'Early Morning Tea' sets, dinner sets, coffee services and even sets for butter rations. This shape still fits in well with today's modern lifestyles.

Poole pieces from the 1950s are among my real favourites. Two of the company's designers, Guy Sydenham and Alfred Read, produced a range during this decade known as 'Freeform', which epitomized the period. Once again, there were many variations, designs and colours produced, and the range proved an instant success with buyers and collectors.

descriptions of the lots they are offering for auction. It is worth remembering that a set of terms and conditions are normally published at the back of most auction catalogues. Listed under the heading of 'Conditions of Business', it is essential to make yourself familiar with these points before you intend to bid in an auction sale.

Never a company to rest on its laurels, Poole began to look for a new direction, and in 1958 Robert Jefferson became the resident designer. Jefferson had trained at the Royal College of Art, and had been a lecturer in ceramics at Stoke-on-Trent College of Art. With extensive experience in ceramics, the modern tradition was maintained at Poole. In the 1960s, Jefferson produced a range of oven-to-table ware and compact stacking tableware. This proved a fairly successful range, but nowhere near as successful as the 'Delphis' studio ware that he produced with Tony Morris. The early examples are dynamic and abstract, featuring bright colours; pieces dating 1963–66 command very high premiums in particular. Each one is marked with the designers' monogram and 'Studio Poole'. The success of the range both in Britain and abroad took Poole by surprise, and a vast number of pieces were produced. In the 1970s, the patterns were simplified, with colours that consisted mainly of red, orange, yellow and green. The range remained a major part of Poole's output and wasn't withdrawn until 1980.

The next Poole range to come into fashion was the 'Aegean' range, which was developed by Leslie Elsden using a darker palette. It was introduced in 1970 as a replacement for Delphis, and, although it proved less popular for Poole, it remained in production until 1980.

If you are interested in Poole pottery, one range that is definitely worth collecting is 'Atlantis'. Dating from the 1970s, this was again inspired by Guy Sydenham.

Poole pottery is a front-runner in modern-day collectables, and represents a good investment. Many of the items produced by Poole today are likely to be collector's items of the future.

Questions Frequently Asked

Anyone new to an auction sale and the running of an auction room will have questions to ask about how it all works. I have been asked countless questions about this subject over the years, and so have listed below some of the most frequently raised queries. Do not to be afraid to ask the auctioneer or his/her staff any of the following questions, or indeed, anything else that you might be unclear about. The myth surrounding an auction room and its buyers will always hang over the antiques trade and it is not until you get into the auction room that you realise just how easy it is to buy or sell at a sale.

Q: What is a reserve price?

A: A reserve price is an amount agreed between the auctioneer and the seller. This figure helps to protect the true value of an item that is entered into an auction. The auctioneer is free to advise you of this figure, but will often ask for a certain amount of discretion when the bidding starts: this is normally agreed at 10 percent of the reserve price. However, some clients insist on a fixed reserve, which would mean that when the auctioneer is taking bids, he has no discretion whatsoever – if the lot does not reach the reserve price, then the lot will be announced as unsold.

Q: Does an auctioneer reveal the reserve price?

A: No. The reserve price is confidential, known only by the auction-eer and the seller. However, the estimate published in the catalogue description will be similar to the reserve price. For example, if an estimate reads £200–£300, then you can probably assume that the reserve price is approximately £180. Auctioneers tend to try and keep the reserve price low so that they can attract as many interested clients as possible. It is far better to have two, three or even four individuals interested in a particular lot, because if people are bidding against each other the lot will stand a greater chance of exceeding the reserve.

Q: What happens if your item is not sold during an auction sale?
A: Some auction houses charge an unsold lot fee. This is sometimes one percent of the low estimate, although it is sometimes as much as 10 percent of the low estimate. This charge is usually printed on your entry form, so it is important that you read this carefully. Many auctioneers do not charge an unsold fee, particularly if the auctioneer has set the reserve price. If the item is unsold, the auctioneer will discuss options for the lot with the client. What often happens is that the unsold item is put for-ward at the next available auction, with its reserve price lowered to the highest bid it attracted in the previous sale.

Q: What happens if my goods are sold at auction but not paid for or collected by the buyer?
A: This scenario is covered in the auctioneer's conditions of sale. Understandably, an auction house cannot pay a client if the buyer has not paid for a lot. As an auctioneer for many years, I discovered that one of the most difficult tasks of the occupation was trying to make sure that buyers paid for goods on time. This enables the auction house to release payment to the sellers and maintain a speedy turnover. Traders and pri-vate buyers usually collect their items within three to five working days. If the goods are not collected within this time, most auction houses will charge a storage fee. This charge can range from £1 per lot to £5 per lot, so collect your purchases on time, particularly if you've made several! This system only tends to break down when goods are sold to specialist collectors who have to arrange shipping and payment from abroad. If there is a hold-up with your payment, the auctioneer will notify you.

There are occasions, however, when goods are not collected or paid for at all. There are a couple of options open to the auctioneer if this scenario occurs. Buying an item at auction forms a legally binding con-tract, which means that the auctioneer can sue the buyer for the amount

95

outstanding. However, it is more likely that after a period of eight weeks the auctioneer will simply advise the client selling the lot to place the item in another sale.

Q: Why do auctioneers charge a buyer's and a seller's premium?

A: Salerooms are like all other businesses: and they need to make money and cover costs. An auction house cannot survive on a single commission charge. There are numerous overheads involved in running a respectable saleroom, which are covered by these charges.

Q: As I am a private buyer and not registered for VAT, do I still have to pay this tax on top of the commission charge?

A: Yes, I am afraid you do. However, VAT is normally only charged on the buyer's and seller's premiums, **not** the total hammer price. For example, if you buy an item for £100 and the buyer's premium is £11.75, including VAT, the tax you have paid is £1.75, or 17.5 percent of £10. Unless you are registered for VAT you cannot claim this amount back.

When a lot is entered into an auction sale by a trader who is registered for VAT, the tax is sometimes payable on both the hammer price and the buyer's premium. If this is the case, the auction house will state this clearly in the catalogue description.

Q: I entered an item into an auction with an estimate of £200–£300, but it was broken at the viewing and it could not be sold at auction. Where do I stand?

A: When entering goods into an auction house you will be given the option to take out insurance. This will cost anything from 1–2.5 percent of the low estimate of the item. If you are unfortunate enough to have an item broken at auction, the saleroom will be able to claim on their insurance and will pay you back the value of the low estimate.

Q: I entered an item into an auction sale with an estimate of £200–£300 and it sold for £450, but was broken after the sale had finished. Am I covered for this damage?

A: Once again, if you have taken out insurance with your auctioneers, you will be covered for the hammer price that the item was sold for if the damage is the fault of the auction house. If the buyer has paid for the lot and has broken it him- or herself while packing it, then he or she is liable for the damage.

Q: I have received a cheque for the lot I sold, but I am disappointed with the amount I've received. I sold goods to the value of £300, but the cheque is for just £150, with transport, insurance, illustration and commission charges taken off. Why is this?

A: You **must** read your entry form thoroughly before you decide to enter any goods into an auction sale. These charges can mount up. An auction house may need to hire a team to collect your goods and clear your house, insure the goods and illustrate the items in their catalogue to ensure maximum exposure to the public. Again, it is crucial that you read the terms and conditions of business before entering any item into an auction sale.

Q IS FOR QUIMPER WARE

Quimper (pronounced 'Kem-pair') is a town in Brittany in north-west France which for centuries has produced a style of tin-glazed earthenware pottery called faïence. The use of the opaque tin glaze is what distinguishes faïence from other types of pottery, and it requires great skill and artistry. Many countries have produced faïence; in the Netherlands it is known as Delftware, whilst pieces from Renaissance Italy are called 'maiolica' (not to be confused with 'Majolica', a trade name of the Minton pottery).

The most famous Quimper pottery was owned by Jules Henriot, whose name and products are synonymous with Quimper ware. The tradition of local faïence production continues in the town today, with two working factories. Although one is controlled by an American company, the other is still owned by descendants of earlier Quimper potters and craftsmen.

The attractive hand-painted pieces from Quimper often depict scenes of Brittany life, and the Celtic influences are instantly recognisable. Many of the earlier pieces show signs of damage due to the delicacy of the earthenware and the glazes. Many collectors have a cut-off date of 1940 for so-called 'vintage Quimper'. This is based on the fact that modern techniques and machinery introduced after the Second World War have resulted in the creation of a different sort of product, which whilst very collectable, is not as fine as that produced before.

Rock and Pop Memorabilia

This is definitely an area in the world of auctions, antiques and collectables in which there are still genuine bargains to be had. Some of the most desirable collectables in this field relate to the giants of rock and pop, including Elvis Presley, Cliff Richard, the Beatles, the Rolling Stones and Jimmy Hendrix, to name but a few. One thing to bear in mind when collecting this sort of memorabilia is that the items making money today are actually over 40 years old.

Beatles for Sale

The Beatles represent the top end of rock and pop memorabilia. At one 2004 auction, the iconic jacket worn by John Lennon on the cover of the album *Sgt Pepper's Lonely Hearts Club Band* sold for over £100,000. John Lennon had given the jacket to a charity shop, where an assistant bought it for £10, as she was a massive fan of the Beatles. This was in the late 1960s, when the Beatles were still together. After ten or so years she decided to sell the jacket at an auction of Beatles' memorabilia and it was consequently sold to a collector for £100. This collector kept the jacket for over 20 years, and what a nice investment it turned out to be.

To further highlight the popularity of the Beatles, let me give you some examples of the prices items relating to the band fetched in 2005. A signed copy of the album *With the Beatles*, signed by all four members of the group, sold for £11,750. A copy of the single 'Love me Do', signed by Paul McCartney, went for £13,500. On average, a complete set of autographs from John, Paul, George and Ringo is worth about £8,000, but when it comes to single signatures, John Lennon's is the most collectable. The ceramics company Royal Worcester made a tray that depicted the Beatles on it, which is now worth £100–£150, and even small, plastic children's guitars with pictures of the Beatles on them are worth £200–£300. In fact, almost anything original relating to the Beatles is worth money.

Like a Rolling Stone

The Rolling Stones is still one of the most exciting British rock bands ever. The fact that they are still together makes their early memorabilia a lot more affordable. A set of four signatures by the original Rolling Stones – Mick Jagger, Brian Jones, Charlie Watts and Keith Richards – is worth between £400–£600. The most valuable of these signatures is that of the now deceased Brian Jones. As far as I am aware, the highest price that a piece of Rolling Stones memorabilia achieved was for a reel-to-reel recording featuring Mick Jagger and Keith Richards that dated back to 1962 – it made a staggering £78,500 at auction. Autographed guitars that belonged to the group tend to make between £1,000–£1,500, and represent a fairly good investment for years to come.

Popular Posters

One area that is still relatively affordable in the realm of pop memorabilia is that of concert posters. Posters ranging from the 1960s to the 1980s can still be acquired for between £100–£500, depending on the group. As mentioned (see page 52), it is also worth looking out for psychedelic album covers from the 1960s.

So, what is going to be the next big thing in pop memorabilia? Items relating to Wham, Abba, Queen and Madonna's early career are moving up in value and, believe or not, I think that objects relating to the Spice Girls have potential for collectors. The group was phenomenally successful, and dolls, bags, clothing and cards were all produced bearing the Spice Girls' logo. Although these were mass-produced, many were discarded. They are extremely affordable now, and will only go up in value. Other bands worth keeping an eye on now are The Darkness and the Scissor Sisters.

Sleepers

'Sleeper' is a term you will hear often in and around auction rooms. The term itself holds no great mystery: it refers to a valuable item that has gone unnoticed, or is of much greater value than the estimate it has been given. Naturally, these objects are among the most highly cherished discoveries for anyone venturing into a saleroom. But, as an auction-goer, how do you recognize or uncover a sleeper?

The presence of a sleeper is nearly always the responsibility of the saleroom, and more often than not their presence boils down to incorrect cataloguing. If you are a regular in an auction room, you are bound to have witnessed an occasion when an object with a catalogue estimate of £50–£100 sells for five, ten or even a hundred times this amount. This will happen if the saleroom has grossly undervalued the item, either through a general lack of knowledge about the item or a lack of infor-mation about current markets.

One place that you may find a sleeper is in a job lot (see pages 62–63), which is usually put together by an auction room when it has cleared the contents of a house. Sometimes the contents that are perceived to be of lesser value are sorted by a junior cataloguer; without the necessary level of experience, it is possible that an object with a value of thousands of pounds can end up on a shelf of items of lesser value that are also included in the job lot. This is why it is so important to dig deep when you come across jobs lots. Of course, you need to have some level of specialist knowledge to recognize a sleeper, but when you do, it can be enormously exciting and extremely profitable. It can also be extremely nerve-racking, as until you start to bid you won't know whether anyone else has spotted the item, or how much they are prepared to pay for it!

One of my greatest discoveries as an art dealer was a sleeper. I remember vividly entering an auction room and discovering an original watercolour by the noted artist Cecil Aldin (1870–1935). However, the catalogue described the work as a print! On closer inspection, I realized that the watercolour was a coaching scene, one of a series of popular scenes illustrated by Aldin.

I realized that this work was worth as much as £3,500, despite the fact that the catalogue estimate was £50–£60. With the help of a friendly bank manager, I approached the auction house confidently the next day, although somewhat weary having suffered a sleepless and anxious night. As the time to bid for the watercolour drew nearer, my heart began to beat faster and faster. I decided to apply a tactical move and asked an amiable porter if he would execute my bid for me. I did this because I knew that people in the saleroom were aware that I was an art dealer, and if they saw me bidding on this 'print' they would smell a rat and start to bid against me. Finally, the time came and the auctioneer announced Lot 326 – a Cecil Aldin print of a coaching scene. With only one bid of £40, my friendly porter upped the price to £50. It was the only bid in the saleroom. The hammer dropped. I could not believe it – despite all the nervous anticipation of the night before and fears of being outbid, the painting was mine – and for just £50. I paid for the watercolour, collected it and took it home where I just stared at it for the next two hours, amazed at how lucky I had been. Later, I placed the work in a specialist sale, where it sold for £3,750!

Is an event like this a rarity? I think that it probably isn't, and I still believe there are sleepers waiting to be discovered in auction houses all over the country.

Although a specialist field – and one that many scholars have spent a lifetime researching – sleepers by the Old Masters can reap rich rewards. This is an area in which even the large, prestigious auction houses can find themselves at fault. Many sleepers are paintings of this ilk, so if your particular area of interest is art, go with your hunches. You never know, you might end up with a Rembrandt!

Sold!

'Sold' is the word which will be most pleasurable to your ears if you are the winning bidder. But when should you start bidding? Once the auc-

S IS FOR SPORTING MEMORABILIA

This is a superb area for collectors, especially if you have a passion for a particular sport, whether it is cricket, golf, motor-racing, horse-racing or fishing.

Sports memorabilia is relatively new to salerooms, and specialist sales have only really begun to occur over the last 20 years. Although these sales often concentrate on the higher end of the market, it is still worth keeping your eyes peeled, as you can sometimes bag a collector's item that will only set you back a few pounds.

One category of sports memorabilia that is worth looking out for at boot sales and antiques fairs is football programmes, particularly from pre-war or international matches, and those that relate to the big clubs, for example Manchester United, Chelsea, Arsenal and Tottenham Hotspur. These are often very affordable items. There is also sometimes good money to be had for the programmes for big friendly matches, especially when a lesser team has played a premier-ship team.

Of course, the 1966 World Cup can prove to be hugely profitable when investing in football memorabilia. For example, the shirt worn by Geoff Hurst in that particular cup final sold at Christie's for £91,750. Then again, he is still the only man to score a hat trick in a World Cup final!

Memorabilia relating to current footballers, such as David Beckham, are definitely a good investment for the future. An England shirt worn by Beckham can sell for £2,000–£3,000.

Golf is a sport with a long history, and its popularity has produced

tioneer has read out the catalogue description, he will suggest a starting bid. Usually this figure will be below the estimate that you see in the catalogue, but do not assume that the auctioneer's starting bid is the lowest price available. If the item has a reserve on it then the auctioneer will have to start below that price in order to encourage the bidders to get above the level of the reserve. As the bidding progresses the auctioneer has the opportunity to sell the item to the highest bidder. It could be you on the day, but on other occasions you may not be so lucky. Knowing when to start bidding is entirely down to the individual buyer, and everyone uses a different technique when bidding in a saleroom.

a wide variety of equipment and items to enthuse collectors. Although antique golfing objects are rare and expensive, there are still plenty of things to look out for that will suit more modest budgets. Old golf clubs are great items to collect, but make sure you inspect them properly before bidding, because it is not worth collecting clubs that display excessive wear and tear. Don't forget to check for woodworm on old clubs, and if a club has an iron head, look out for rust. You should never be tempted to clean antique golf clubs, as this decreases their value. Instead, leave this job to specialist restorers.

Fishing items are a recent addition to the market for collectables, but it is a fast-growing niche. Items by the top manufacturers of fishing equipment, for example, Hardy's, will set you back thousands of pounds, but there are many obscure objects that can be snapped up for a few pounds. To understand more about the subject, it is worth investing in a few old fishing tackle catalogues, as they will highlight many collectable items.

Preserved and mounted fish can fetch bundles of money, depending on the quality of the taxidermy, the size and species of the fish, and when it was caught. When looking for this sort of object, keep an eye out for the names F. W. Anstiss and J. Copper & Sons.

If, like me, you want to anticipate the next collector's items in the sporting world, then aim to acquire items from upcoming important events such as the Olympics, the Football World Cup and FA Cup Final matches.

Traders or dealers in the auction room normally start the bidding off as soon as the auctioneer drops to a price below the estimate in the catalogue; this is an old trick, used to gain the attention of the auctioneer in the hope that a moment's loss of concentration will mean a bargain is obtained. These dealers will bid without even looking at the item. Try not to fall into this trap, as many people have lost a lot of money by buying something below the estimate and thinking they had got themselves a bargain.

Time to Sell

Is there ever a right time to sell anything? Certain factors certainly contribute to the timing of this important element of collecting antiques. Let's imagine that you've been building a personal collection that consists of items from lower price brackets, and that over a period of years these items have increased in value. You now have the opportunity to secure an item that will enhance your collection – this is the perfect time to sell off some of the less valuable pieces and continue to build your collection around the better examples. For me, this is one of the most exciting aspects of collecting antiques, because as you build your collection you constantly gain knowledge, and with this comes that all-important thing: profit. When you reach this point with your collection, you will know whether new items you come across are worth investing in. For example, you'll be able to determine whether an item has been restored, or whether it has the correct markings. Once you feel confident with this aspect of collecting, you'll then realize that it's time to start upgrading.

Trends

If you study the antiques market and subscribe to the weekly magazines available on the subject, you will come to realize that antiques follow certain trends. Following these trends can reap good profits, as you will generally find that the first signs of these trends occur in the major salerooms.

Once you are aware of a burgeoning trend, you'll need to get going

T IS FOR TYPEWRITERS

If I had a pound for every person who has brought a typewriter into my saleroom over the years and asked how much it was worth I would be a rich man. Ninety-nine percent of the time, these machines are worth no more than £20, as they were mass-produced. However, there are some rare exceptions.

Typewriters were first patented in 1867 and early or unusually shaped machines are usually worth more than the norm. In 1952 the writer Ian Fleming commissioned New York's Royal Typewriter Company to make him a gold-plated typewriter. This example, a rarity to be sure, later sold at auction for a record price of £50,000.

Another typewriter that's in a different league is the Malling Hansen Writing Ball, which was created in 1867 by the director of Denmark's Deaf and Dumb Institute. Only 180 were made and each one is now worth up to £50,000.

and visit some of the provincial salerooms to see what bargains you can pick up. When you compare regional prices to those in London, you may be pleasantly surprised to discover, for example, that you can pick up an item that sold in a London saleroom for £1,200 for a quarter of that price in a provincial saleroom. However, to adopt this tactic, you have to be quick and on the ball, as there will be other people out there playing this game.

In many ways the antiques business is like the world of fashion. It really is just one continuing circle; as one item comes out of fashion, so another takes its place. Art Deco was extremely popular ten years ago, for example. Every house seemed to have a piece of Art Deco china, furniture or something from the period. Then suddenly Deco was out, and it became very fashionable to collect modern and contemporary furniture. With time and experience you will almost certainly manage to stay ahead of the game and anticipate these trends. Some of the most successful dealers and traders are those who have a small knowledge of many fields. By attending many salerooms and antiques fairs they pick up on the trends and make their profits by buying and selling at a relatively low profit margin, say 10–30 percent. This works because their turnover is high, and they certainly keep their heads above water.

T IS FOR TOYS

The fashion for collecting toys has increased dramatically over the past 15 years. One of the primary reasons for this is nostalgia, with many people feeling they can hark back to their childhood by building a collection of toys. This is a vast area, and includes teddy bears, trains, cars, planes, clockwork toys, tin-plate toys and dolls. Modern toys – for example, early computer games – are also becoming highly collectable.

When it comes to toy vehicles, there is a plethora of names to look out for, including Hornby, Tri-ang, Dinky, Corgi, Matchbox, Lesney, Meccano, Schuco, Chad Valley and Tonka. Corgi is one of my particular favourites. The company was founded in the 1950s, as a subsidiary of Mettoy, and it was named, believe it or not, after the Queen's favourite breed of dog. Corgi was the first company to really market its toys, advertising the products on television as early as 1957. Corgi cars had boots, bonnets, doors and plastic windows that opened. The company produced some classic items, including the Chipperfield Circus gift set, which was issued in 1964, and a replica of the TV fox Basil Brush seated in a car, which was issued in 1971. This piece, which played the character's catchphrase 'Boom! Boom!' is now worth £150–£200 in good condition. As is the case with all toys, if you have the original box and packaging, this will enhance the price. Many toys are purchased by adults without any intention of using them for the purpose for which they were created; instead they are bought for investment – and what a cracking investment some of these turn out to be.

The Dinky company started by modelling miniatures in 1930. These vehicles catered for the affordable die-cast market, as they were a lot cheaper than the costly tin-plate versions. Dinky toys were popular with children from the 1940s to the 1980s. Colour variations in the products make a difference to the value, and unusual items seem to reach good prices; for instance, the lawnmower, which was produced in 1950, and the Dinky model of the Avro York Airliner, which was issued from 1946–49 and is now worth about £90. Although hundreds of Dinky Morris Oxfords were issued, one rare model, a two-tone edition in blue and white that was issued in 1954, is now worth £700–£900. The original version dates from 1937, and only three are known to exist.

Dinky also produced quite a large range of toys based on commercial vehicles. These were expensive in their day, and are expensive now, especially when they are in good condition and boxed. The most sought after Dinky toy is the Bentalls van, which is named after the department store. An example of this rare green van, which has distinctive yellow panels and a white roof, sold at an auction recently for over £12,000. It is worth mentioning that you need to be aware that some people do try to over-paint these items to make them look and appear more rare than they really are.

Matchbox cars are also very collectable. Some of the early American models can make four figures at auctions. Some 1960s examples that are boxed and in good condition can make between £100–£200.

Toy collecting is a very exciting field, but as with any specialist area, you need to do your homework first, read up on the subject and make sure you are making the right decisions when you intend to buy. I think there will always be a profit to be made from something that displays craftsmanship, so look out for the better-made items, keep all the packaging and try to keep to one theme. Cult films or television shows that have an accompanying range of merchandise are usually a sound investment.

Understanding Antiques

I cannot stress enough how important it is that you understand the commitment you face when investing in antiques or building a collection. It's important to remember not to rush into anything – slow and steady always wins the race. If you are unsure about an item, then trust your instincts. Even experts make mistakes, and you can avoid costly errors by following that simple rule I mentioned earlier – look, listen and learn.

Only after you have gained a certain amount of confidence in and around salerooms and antiques fairs should you start putting your hands in your pockets. Advice is always going to be on hand if you are unsure about a particular lot or item, so do not be afraid to ask questions. You will only be able to bid with confidence once you have gained a certain amount of knowledge about the category of antiques that you're interested in. Before you reach this level of understanding, you should always seek advice from reputable dealers.

Putting Your Trust in Dealers

Most specialist dealers have a vast knowledge of their chosen subject, and you can normally buy from them with complete confidence. A good dealer will provide you with the provenance of the item and its history, and will inform you of any restoration work that has been undertaken on the piece. And if there's a problem with your purchase, you can always go back to the dealer and ask for advice. For example, if you were to buy an extending dining table and then discover, when you get it home, that one of the leaves is a bit sticky when you wind it out, but you can't fathom how to fix it, you can return to the dealer and ask for help in solving this problem. This is not the case, however, with goods bought at auction – once you've paid for an item and taken it home, you're on your own (except in the case of incorrect catalogue descriptions; see page 90).

If you become friendly with a particular antiques dealer, that dealer will normally advise you about any other items you intend to buy. Furthermore, if you ever decide to build on your collection, or seek out additional items, the dealer will normally aim to help you source items and give you a good deal.

When buying from an antiques dealer it is advisable to stick to businesses that are part of LAPDA (London and Provincial Antique Dealers Association Ltd). This organization provides representation for dealers in the antiques and fine art trade who meet its requirements in terms of knowledge, experience and commercial reliability. The association welcomes enquiries from the trade and the public, and will take appropriate action if it discovers that its rules of practice have been breached, or if there is a dispute involving one of its members.

BADA (The British Antique Dealers Association Ltd) was established in 1918. This is also a superb organization, which not only sets up regular exhibitions but also runs one- and two-year courses in restoration. Another name that deserves a mention is the Society of Fine Art Auctioneers (SOFAA), which is a professional body that represents British auctioneers in this field. The society insists on the very highest standards for its members, so that vendors always receive the best possible service.

Affiliation with any or all of these associations is worth looking out for when you approach dealers, as you know that they have to apply certain standards to their business transactions, and that you have recourse for arbitration if anything goes wrong.

Under-bidding

One of the most frustrating things that can happen at an auction is to leave the sale as the under-bidder. As my friend and colleague David Dickinson always says – never go home as the bridesmaid. There are several ways to avoid this situation. The first is to carry on bidding whatever happens, thus ensuring that you go home with the lot you came for. However, if you do this then you will find yourself on dangerous ground, and might end up paying more for an item than it is actually worth. If you want to avoid under-bidding, then I would recommend the following guidelines.

Traders normally bid in round figures; for example, £100, £150, £200, £250 etc. This allows them to follow a simple price structure when buying and selling goods. If you find yourself bidding against a trader, and the bid ends up with him or her at £100, I think it is worth pushing your bid up an extra £10 to secure the lot.

If you leave a commission bid, for example, £100, remember to write '+ 1 bid' on the form, which means the auctioneer will automatically bid an extra £10 on your behalf – nine times out of ten that will be enough to secure the lot.

When you visit a saleroom and mark your catalogue with your bid limit for a particular lot, don't be too put off if you are outbid for items that are common to the saleroom. Some objects have a standard price, unless they are a little more unusual. If this is the case, then this is where your knowledge of the market will kick in. If a collectable is rarely seen in an auction room, but the estimate given by the auctioneer screams 'come and buy me' at just £300–£500, then you can guarantee that there will be several other people interested in purchasing the lot. In a situation like this you have to keep your wits about you and decide exactly how much you are going to pay, and whether you are willing and able to add the extra bids to secure the items. As you bid, look around the saleroom to see who the competition is and whether you know them. Is this bidder a specialist trader or another private buyer? All these factors will help you decide whether or not you should extend your bid. If it is a general trader or a specialist collector, then you probably should. If it is a private buyer, you should be more cautious. In some cases, a bidding war can break out between two private buyers that takes an object well beyond its value to anyone but these individuals. When the hammer finally drops after a conflict like this, the price is usually shocking to all present.

I witnessed such a scenario myself when conducting a sale a few years ago. One lot was a modern dining table and chairs with a matching sideboard. It had an estimate of £80–£120. It transpired that two families had fallen out over the estate from which it came, and both thought they were entitled to granddad's furniture. The retail value for these items was about £550. The bidding slowly rose from £150 to £300 to £500 to £700, before finally ending up at £1,100, ten times the estimate. You can imagine the shock in the auction room. This is a classical example of auction fever, as neither bidder was going to back down, however ridiculous the price. However, this case did have a happy ending. After the sale, the two families decided to keep the table and chairs in one house and the sideboard in the other. It was a costly lesson for them both.

U IS FOR UNUSUAL LOTS

Buying unusual lots can be a safe way to make a profit. Anything in an antiques sale which stands out as unusual will always attract a lot of attention. By keeping your finger on the pulse in a particular specialist field you will be able to decide whether or not a particular item is unusual and worth going for. Many auction houses do not have expertise in all fields and so this is where your knowledge will kick in. For example, if you are a Beswick collector and collect the animal figures, you will be aware of the different colourways which are available. We once had a Beswick fish entered in our sale. As the auctioneer, I catalogued it accordingly and gave it the normal estimate for a Beswick fish on stand of £80–£120. It was not until just before the viewing that I was inundated with emails and phone calls regarding the colourways of the fish. The same question was asked repeatedly: was I confident that these were the correct colourways? Having established that the colourways were different to the ones listed, it transpired that this particular fish was a prototype and only a very few were known to exist. Beswick fish figurines normally reach £120, but this particular item sold for £800.

It is not only different colourways that attract attention. Unusual shapes and designs are worth looking out for, too. One area where such items turn up time and time again is with toys. Advertising ware is also a favoured collecting field. Other favourites include small snuff boxes, vesta cases, trays, tobacco jars and lids, toast racks, teapots, egg cups, tea caddies, smoker's companions, sporting memorabilia and paperweights. One of the great pleasures of uncommon antiques is that they make excellent conversation pieces. Whether you are entertaining at home or trying to attract customers to your antique shop or stall, these items stand out in the crowd. The good news is that the price will definitely reflect this special quality.

Valuations

Getting the correct valuation for any antique or work of art is just as important as knowing how much to pay for an item. Obtaining the right valuation is quite easy if you follow a few simple guidelines.

Let's assume that you have inherited a work of art, and you are not sure of its true value. Where is the best place to find out the value of this item? Like the second-hand car market, many everyday objects sold in the antiques trade have a set price range. For example, if you have a Victorian bun chest with two short drawers and three long drawers, the chances are that your valuation is going to be between £80–£120; if you have a Georgian chest of drawers with two short drawers and three long drawers, then it will probably be valued at £180–£250. Items like these tend to form the staple diet of all auction rooms. So to get a valuation on an everyday object, all you usually need to do is call a local saleroom.

But what if you have got something that is a bit more unusual? You might have a quick flip through your reference books and see similar items that are worth quite a lot of money. How do you know that your item is worth a similar price? This is when you need to be on your toes. Start by consulting your local saleroom to see what they think. However, as certain items seem to do better in specific salerooms, it is worth seeking the opinions of another two or three salerooms.

The easiest way to do this is to take a photograph of the item and send it to the salerooms by which you wish to have the object valued. One thing you must remember when getting a valuation from an auction house is that they are giving you a price based on what they think the item would make at auction, which is not the same as the replacement value you are given with an insurance valuation (see pages 58–59). It is also important to understand that the estimate given by a saleroom is guesswork to a degree, as the price you will get for an item will depend on various factors, including who is in the saleroom on the day the lot goes on sale.

When selecting the auction house in which you intend to sell your goods, it is always wise to have a chat with someone who has sold lots through the same business. Most auction rooms have a quick turn-around on general items, and within a month of entering your goods into a saleroom the items should be sold.

Don't forget that you will have to pay various charges when you sell through an auction house, as described on pages 28 and 44–45. It is certainly worth bearing these costs in mind when you sell a run-of-the-mill item, as you may not end up with a great deal of cash once these charges have been deducted. If you feel that the auction isn't going to provide you with the best price, you can always approach a trader to sell your goods for you once you have received an estimate. You may get a better price from a trader because he or she may realize that your items are new to the market, and that they won't have to compete with other traders in the saleroom. I would only recommend this course of action, however, if your item or object has a value of £500 or less.

Selling Art

If are selling a painting, then you should do some groundwork so that you can establish where you are going to gain maximum profit or the best market price. If, for instance, you live in Kent and your painting is a landscape of the Sussex Downs, then it probably makes sense to sell your painting in a saleroom in that county. A transaction like this can easily be set up: you simply need to email or post a photograph of your item to a selection of auction houses in the area that you deem most appropriate to sell your painting, and they will send you back a valuation. You might find that you're pleasantly surprised at the difference it makes to sell a painting in the area that it depicts. It is also worth bearing in mind that many salerooms have excellent websites and databases that include clients on the lookout for particular lots

Locating the area in which you wish to sell your item is quite straightforward using the standard auction reference books. Most auction rooms also have websites, which can help you find the right saleroom.

V IS FOR VALENTINE CARDS

Being an old romantic, I think that this is definitely a field that is great to collect. Like postcards, Valentine cards are part of a collectables category known as 'ephemera'. What is significant about these particular cards is that they are actually quite rare, and you may be pleasantly surprised at what some cards are worth.

Messages built around romantic verses have been exchanged between couples for many centuries. One of the first references to Valentine's Day was in the diaries of Samuel Pepys, which were written in the 1660s. Some very early Valentine cards were engraved and coloured by hand, with subjects that varied from flowers and cherubs to religious themes.

Handmade Valentine cards from the 19th century are certainly worth looking out for. These examples were often fashioned from embossed paper, with decorations such as lace, silk, ribbons, shells or even trinkets. A few lines of romantic poetry were usually included. Some of these early cards are worth £40–£120 today.

Towards the end of the 19th century, a technique called chromolithography was invented. This is a form of colour printing in which the end product looks very similar to a watercolour. As a result of this innovation, printed Valentine cards replaced hand-made versions. For the wealthy of the period, boxed cards were also introduced. Often decorated with silver and gold lace, some of the more expensive cards also contained a small pendant or even a seed pearl. The verses and messages included in these cards can tell you a lot about the historical period in which they were produced, and their inclusion enhances the desirability of the card. Cards that come in original envelopes and bear postmarks are also of greater value.

Some of the early cards are quite cheap, costing between £2–£4. These particular cards are quite unique and are certainly appealing, so why not go out and find an antique Valentine card to send to your loved one on February 14th?

Always be wary of auction houses that do not publish catalogues, as your goods should be on view to as many prospective buyers as possible.

One final piece of advice is that when looking for valuations, you should always use your common sense and only sell with a company you feel happy doing business with.

Not all valuations will be the same

Different valuations for the same object can be a cause for concern, but it's important to look at the reasons why they occur. In other words, you must understand all aspects of the antique you are hoping to sell. The fact that there may be a difference in either the reserve prices or the valuations given by different valuers does not mean that the final price will be dissimilar – when it comes to be sold, it will be down to the buyers at the sale to determine what it is 'worth' on the day.

Many auction houses will want to get your item entered into their sale at the lowest possible price. Not only does this give the auction house an improved chance of securing a sale for you, but it also allows them to offer the item in their catalogue at a 'come-and-buy-me' estimate, which serves as a magnet for other buyers. As a rule, if the valuer thinks your lot would raise £250 he would like to have an estimate of, say, £150–£250. It is very hard to judge what a true market price is in an auction, as individual days can be as different as chalk and cheese. On many occasions I have seen the same object sold on different auction days for varied amounts, but one thing is constant: you need Lady Luck on your side, as well as a good auctioneer. At the end of the day, you should do some groundwork to find out when and where is the best time to sell your goods.

Revised valuations occur from time to time, but these can only be done with your consent and the auction house must inform you if they have found a reason to lower or – sometimes – raise the estimate. Occasionally a restoration or a small hairline crack may have been overlooked, or the object could even turn out to be a fake. Clearly in such cases the value would be reduced. However, it could also become apparent that the lot is more uncommon than first thought, and that its value is therefore higher. Many auction houses do wide-ranging research into the lots prior to their being entered into the catalogue, so they should be able to give potential buyers all the information they need to bid with confidence.

What to Buy Now

Being an antiques expert is sometimes like being a doctor, as you're always being asked your advice, even on your day off. Not that I mind, because antiques are one of my great passions. But there is one question that I am asked more often than any other – what area of antiques should I be collecting now? The answer to that question is not simple, and it would take an entire book to cover every area of investment. But as history has shown, there are many different items that will make you money when it comes to antiques.

Fifteen years ago, I was tipping the Delphi range by Poole (see pages 92–93), a colourful collection of ceramics that was produced in the 1960s and 1970s. Each item was hand-painted, and some studio pieces were unique. Back then, you could acquire Delphi pieces for £5–£40, but they are so popular now that you would have to add a zero to the end of these prices! However, like all things that rise rapidly in the antiques world, these items will reach a peak, and prices may even tumble, so knowing when to sell is as important as knowing when to buy.

Investing in antiques can be enormous fun as well as financially rewarding. Collecting something that seems cheap now is probably the best place to begin your investment, and I think it is highly possible that elaborately decorated objects may make a comeback, after years of stark, minimalist objects proving so popular.

W IS FOR WEST GERMAN POTTERY

Why not invest £200 in one of my top tips: West German ceramics from the 1950s, 1960s and 1970s. These three decades spawned some great items that were produced in vivid, instantly recognizable colours and objects of all shapes and sizes, including jugs, vases and a few more unique designs.

Many have a distinctive 'volcanic' look, with patterns including swirls and spiders' webs. However, there are also plain, mono-chrome vases that are embossed with geometric designs. Although many German companies produced ceramics during this period, there are still a few prominent names to look out for that may sell well in the future, including Bay and Steuler, Ruscha, Jopeko and Sgrafo. Many items by these names can be bought for under £20, but that will not last for long, as people are catching on fast to the increasing value of these pieces.

Some of the best places to look for these ceramics are boot fairs, jumble sales, charity shops and antiques fairs, although if you don't have access to any of these you could try eBay (see pages 86–89). Go for the very brightly coloured vases and jugs, but look closely at the decorations as the quality will vary; try to steer clear of any damaged items and always check for hairline cracks. This can be done with a quick flick of the thumb – if the pot sounds 'dead' then the chances are that it has a crack somewhere.

Wasting Money

Many books on antiques and auctions tell you how to make money and what you should invest in. I don't, however, think that there are many books that will tell you what they think is a waste of money. I do not mind putting my reputation on the line to tell you what items I think are a complete waste of money and should not be bought at auction.

Some of the best bargains can be had at a general sale, but so can the most worthless of items. These sorts of auctions are not catalogued, and you will have to use your own expertise when viewing these sales. Many of them have a varying range of lots, from electric cookers to Georgian chests of drawers. Unless you know your stuff well, you are entering a minefield.

W IS FOR WADE

Wade's 'Whimsies' are something of a phenomenon in the world of antiques and collecting. Many a collector has started off by collecting the ceramic animals produced in this series.

Wade was founded in 1824 by John Wade, a cabinet-maker, and his wife, Anne. By 1830 the couple had begun to dabble in pottery. After John Wade's death in 1859, his son, Joseph, took over the business and worked in the pottery full-time. The company went through various changes of name and personnel throughout the rest of the 19th century and the early 20th century, before becoming known as Wade Potteries in 1939.

It was in the 1940s, when Anthony Wade became one of the company's directors, that Wade really began to hit its stride. The company produced a number of comical animal models. While initial reaction to these was not very encouraging, Anthony Wade was determined not to give up on the idea, and in 1953 he decide to exhibit a set of the models – which included a horse, a poodle, a spaniel, a stag and a squirrel – at the British Industries Fair. From this point on, Whimsies, as the animal ceramics were known, became a major success story.

Anthony Wade then decided to employ a designer and modeller named Bill Harper to come up with some new Whimsies. It was largely due to his efforts that the success of these models continued. It was important to maintain both the price – about 3 shillings in pre-decimal currency – and the quality. Some designs were reproduced over a hundred thousand times from a single mould.

Electrical goods and furniture

If you go to a general auction looking for electrical goods, you should make sure that any item you are interested in has a certificate confirming that it can be sold in the sale. Take care, as, after all, what do you really know about the history of this sort of object? It could have been taken from a house clearance, or it may just have been bought in by a scrap dealer who drives around houses clearing hoovers, fridges, freezers, TVs and video recorders. Personally, I would not recommend that you purchase an item like this at a general auction.

118

In many respects, the 1950s were a golden era for Wade. One important factor of the success of the series was the huge marketing campaign that supported the brand – Wade was one of the first ceramics companies to use television to advertise its products. Whimsies first appeared during a programme called *What's New?*, accompanied by a special jingle. The boxed set promoted on television was called 'TV Pet', with animals based on a popular children's programme. Anthony Wade also made a deal with Walt Disney, a very successful partnership that resulted in the company producing many models of Walt Disney characters.

All models were initially sold as complete boxed sets, and it was not until later that the animal figures were sold individually. Between 1953–59, ten sets of Whimsies, all boxed, were produced. There were less of the first five boxed sets produced, so these tend to be more expensive and collectable. These early sets are now worth £70–£150 – not a bad investment for 3 shillings and sixpence!

In 1983 Wade produced a set of five piggy banks for the National Westminster Bank. A complete set is now worth £160–£180. It is without a doubt a name to keep your eye on, and you won't go far wrong if you decided to invest or trade in Wade. Whimsies can still be picked up for £1–£5, and building a set can be great fun, particularly for younger collectors. However, there's much more to the company than Whimsies, and it is relatively easy to find out more about the brand from the many books on the subject (see pages 155–156).

Sofas and chairs crop up all the time in auctions, along with double beds, but – and it is a big but – items matching this description must have a fire mark. This is a circle with a crossed-out cigarette in the centre that indicates the item is fireproof. It is actually illegal to sell items without this fire mark. You should therefore steer clear of items that don't bear this sign.

Reproduction items

The Far East has reproduced many collectable and highly sought-after

W IS FOR WRITING ACCESSORIES

Fountain pens are another area of antiques in which you can make some money if you learn what to look out for. These writing implements are often overlooked by dealers and auctioneers, and are usually put into job lots, although you can sometimes find examples that have been left in desks or bureaux.

One of the most famous names in pen history is John Jacob Parker, who patented his version of the fountain pen in 1832. Pens made by the American firm L. E. Waterman are also among the most popular for collectors today. This company developed the safety pen, which was designed to prevent the ink from leaking. Collections of 19th-century pens can make big money; as well as Parker and Waterman, look out for names like Conway Stewart and Eversharp.

Multi-coloured pens from the 1930s–50s are worth looking out for, as are limited editions, which were very often produced by Parker. The 1981 Royal Wedding pen, produced in a limited edition of 1,000 to commemorate the wedding of Prince Charles and Lady Diana Spencer, now sells for £500–£600. A limited-edition Parker 75 pen, created for Queen Elizabeth II's Silver Jubilee, is worth up to £600 in today's market.

As with any collectable, it is important to know where to look for bargains. Pens are easy to identify, as the make and the model are usually engraved on the nib, the main body of the pen or the ink cartridge, although you may need to use a magnifying glass to find these. Avoid damaged pens, as this can affect the price by as much as 90 percent. There is no doubt that pens are very collectable now, and some major salerooms hold specialist sales devoted to this category. If you keep your eyes peeled, you may just make a few pounds.

antiques on a mass scale over the years. In an un-catalogued general sale, you will find numerous such items scattered around waiting for an uneducated buyer. I am not saying that it is wrong to collect mass-produced reproduction items like Wade, Sylvac, Staffordshire or the like, but you must be aware of the price you pay for a reproduction item – and bear in mind that its value will rarely increase.

PLATE 17

PREVIOUS PAGE:
A typical specialist silver dealer's stall. This one is only offering flatware, but there's nowhere better to go if you need to fill gaps in your canteen of cutlery.
ABOVE: Never be afraid to have a rummage. The most surprising finds turn up on stalls just like this one!
LEFT: The restorer starts his job. This is highly skilled work, but always remember to get a quote before things get underway.
OPPOSITE: MH in action in the saleroom, checking over the lots.

PLATE 18

PLATE 19

ABOVE: *Leather-bound books look great on open bookshelves. If not collectors' items individually, they are frequently sold by the yard or in job lots.*
LEFT: *Stylized items of furniture from the 1950s and 60s are becoming the new antiques. Keep an eye out for them.*
OPPOSITE: *Copies of vintage magazines can turn up anywhere and often as job lots. Look through them carefully, in particular keeping an eye out for early photographs of celebrities and film stars.*

PLATE 20

PLATE 22

ABOVE: MH in his favourite place: on the rostrum with the gavel!
RIGHT: Once the deal is done, it's time to hand over the cash. Always remember to haggle before agreeing a price.
OPPOSITE: Toy motor vehicles from the mid- and late 20th century are extremely collectable nowadays. Car boot sales are good places to hunt for them.

PLATE 23

ABOVE LEFT: *Top-quality teddy bears command top prices, but even rather weary specimens, such as this 1961 model, are worth a look and can be restored.*

ABOVE RIGHT: *Street stalls are a good place to seek out bargains and unusual objects.*

LEFT: *Prints and drawings have enduring appeal, but it's always good to special-ize in a particular field.*

PLATE 24

Other reproduction items you will find at general sales include those made from bronze, brass and copper. The quality of these sorts of items is so inferior to the originals that they will be quite easy to spot. For example, if you are buying a bronze group and you see a mould line down the back of the item, you can guarantee that it has been mass-produced rather than finely crafted. If you come across one of these items, turn it upside down and look inside. If it is aged, you need to ask how it has became so – it is quite possible that it has been deliberately aged to trick you into thinking it is an antique.

Of course, not all dealers are out to trick or cheat buyers. Most are honest, and will tell you if an item you are interested in is a reproduction. The price on the item will also indicate its provenance to you. Just remember that in an auction that is not catalogued, you will have to decide for yourself what exactly you are buying.

Another type of item that often turns up at auction houses and antiques fairs is the limited-edition cabinet plate. These ceramics are normally boxed, and include certificates. Plates matching this description are usually mass-produced, and although the limited edition might be 10 of 1,000, you will have no way of knowing how many editions of each design have been made – there could be 10 editions, all of which contained 1,000 numbered plates. Collecting limited edition plates like these was very popular in the 1980s, and many households signed up to be sent one plate a month to build up a collection. However, for the reason mentioned above, this is definitely an area that I suggest you steer clear of.

The 'X' Factor

The 'X' factor is the sixth sense that kicks in and tells you when to buy and sell your antiques. While this instinct really only comes with time, there are some golden rules and tricks of the trade that can help you develop this sixth sense by building that extra layer of expertise. Following these rules will also help you avoid the mistakes that many people make when buying and selling at auction. Here are a few things to remember and think about when you attend an auction:

- Always view the lot you're interested in **before** you bid on it. If you cannot view it in person, and you intend to bid by phone or leave a commission bid (see pages 21–22), make sure you ask for a report on the condition of the item.
- Bid with confidence, but don't get carried away and bid more than you intended to – avoid auction fever at all costs (see pages 132–133).
- If you are a trader, always think about profit, not passion.
- Unless a lot is unique, remember that another one will probably turn up one day – so don't get disheartened if you lose an item to another bidder.
- If a dinner or tea service is a couple of items short, you will get it for a cheaper price. You will also have great fun sourcing the missing elements in other salerooms.
- Silver is a great investment and it is very hard to fake.
- If you are selling on a stall at an antiques fair or in a shop, remember: display well to sell well.
- 'All that glisters is not gold' – if a piece of 'gold' has no hallmark,

you will need to test it properly.

- Never be afraid to ask the auctioneer for his or her advice.
- Check the saleroom's buyer's premium, which will vary from 10–25 percent. Don't forget that you may also have to add VAT.
- Don't just base your bids on books that include price guides, as quality and condition are always important factors when it comes to determining what something will cost.
- Do not feel that you are unlucky; you always make your own luck.
- If you are going to buy a lot that needs restoration, you should check the cost of the restoration before you bid on that item.
- Remember that if an item has already been restored, its value will be less than that of an untouched object.
- An item that has been made up of various pieces of furniture, known in the trade as a 'marriage', will be cheaper. These are sometimes difficult to spot, so look closely at furniture that consists of more than one element and see how well the pieces fit together.
- Always go with your instinct, and remember – first impressions are nearly always right.
- You can restore and repair most things, with the exception of glass.
- Never buy antiques or collectables without getting a receipt.
- Always haggle when buying at a fair or in a shop, as most traders will give a 10 percent discount; some will drop even more from the price.
- It is cheaper to buy later in the day at an antiques fair, but to ensure the best choice, get there early.
- If you are starting a collection, stick to one particular area and concentrate on learning as much as you can about your chosen subject – you will be an expert before you know it.
- If you want to maximize your profit with a collection of items, sell the items together at a specialist auction.
- Make sure that you get two or three opinions about the value of an item before you sell it, to ensure that you get a fair price.
- Modern household furniture and fittings can be bought at general auction sales more cheaply than in a shop – you could end up furnishing your house for £500 or less. However, beware when buying electrical goods – don't be afraid to ask for an item to be plugged in and tested, especially televisions or refrigerators, as most are sold as seen.
- Sometimes a picture frame can be worth more than the painting or print it surrounds.
- If you want to invest in antiques, make sure you are aware of current trends. If an item is in vogue, then it will cost more; if an item is

not so fashionable, it will be cheaper, and so it may have more investment potential.

• If an item of silver-coloured jewellery has a small gold tip on its clasp, it may be set in platinum.

• Becoming an antiques dealer is easy, but making a profit is hard – keep a close eye on your profit margin.

• Stick to what you know when bidding, as costly mistakes can be made with impulse buys.

• Antiques are a window on the past. Don't forget that in their day they were contemporary, and that they capture a moment in history.

• You can never stop learning about antiques, as there is always something new to the market.

• Make yourself known to the auctioneer, and he or she will guide you in the right direction.

• Try to tip the porters if they are helpful; you will be amazed at the information they can give you about the saleroom and the lots for sale.

• If you are buying a large item, check the delivery cost first, particularly for something awkward to transport, such as a piano.

• Charity shops are a great source for vintage clothing and collectables.

• Don't dwell on 'the one that got away' – stay positive and think about the one you're going to catch.

• Remember all dealers and traders need to survive, so don't begrudge them their profit.

• Don't be afraid to invest in modern furniture – a lot of money has been made by investors who have taken this path.

• If you wear designer labels, then keep hold of them, as top names like Vivienne Westwood, Alexander McQueen, Dolce and Gabbana and Versace will almost certainly reap a profit one day.

• Modern technology is becoming more and more collectable, so keep hold of those old mobile phones and hand-held computer games.

• If you want to collect blue-and-white china and display it on your dressers, there are many designs other than the ever-popular Willow Pattern to collect. Always keep your eyes open for unusual shapes and designs, particularly those that highlight animals such as dogs and rabbits.

• Remember to rummage when you visit a general auction sale or boot fair; you'll be amazed at the bargains you could find lurking at the bottoms of boxes.

• If you want to collect jewellery, make sure you invest in a diamond tester – it may cost you a few pounds up-front, but I guarantee it will help you turn a profit one day.

• If you need to research items you have viewed at a sale, most local libraries have an area dedicated to antiques and collectables. London's Victoria and Albert Museum has one of the world's largest reference libraries. It is dedicated to art, antiques and artefacts, with experts on hand to advise you.

• Before you set off on your merry travels to an auction room it is always worth obtaining a catalogue to make sure the goods for sale are what you are looking for.

• At certain auction rooms sales can be subject to cancellation at short notice. It is therefore wise to check that the sale is still on before you make a long journey.

• It is imperative that you inspect goods thoroughly at an auction house, as some are sold without any guarantees. If the goods are sold with faults, it is wise to check that they can be easily repaired.

• Catalogues are not set in stone and the list of items can change. If an item is broken, damaged or deemed to be mis-catalogued, it will also be withdrawn.

• When you are at the auction sale listen out for the auctioneer describing the lots you are interested in, as sometimes the description may change.

• If you bid by mistake on the wrong lot, you must inform the auctioneer immediately. This will give the auctioneer the opportunity to re-offer the lot there and then. Be warned that this is, however, entirely at the auctioneer's discretion. Always remember that a successful bid at an auction carries legal obligations.

• One other thing people are not aware of is how cold some auction rooms can be in winter. Make sure you wrap up warmly!

• If you are bidding on a lot which you are not sure will fit into your vehicle, take a tape measure to check in advance that it will fit.

• It is worth bearing in mind that all electrical goods purchased from an auction sale will be sold without guarantee.

• If you decide to buy a car or van from an auction sale be sure to check it thoroughly. Do not be afraid to ask your local garage for advice; they might even be able to help you with an inspection.

• If you are a successful phone or commission bidder in an auction which is far from where you live, always check how much the packing and delivery will be and reflect this cost in the amount you intend to bid.

• And last, but not least – happy hunting!

You Should Think About The Future

I have been an auctioneer and valuer of antiques for over 25 years. During this time I have seen many fads and trends come and go, and I have become familiar with the things that regularly crop up in auction rooms. With this valuable experience in hand, I would like to present an A to Z of antiques and collectables that I think will prove to be good investments for the future. Some of the items are modern, dating only to the 20th century, however, I feel strongly that this is the one of the last remaining areas in which you can bag a bargain. Collecting antiques is often fuelled by nostalgia, and many people want to collect items that they remember from their younger days, as it imbues them with a sense of familiarity.

Conversely, Victorian and Georgian furniture and antiques have fallen out of favour due to the fashion for loft living and the division of larger houses into flats. Dark chests of drawers, large wardrobes, scroll-ended chaise longues and extending Victorian dining tables and chairs do not work well in these new loft spaces. As a result, many individuals are looking back to the 1950s and 1960s to build their collections. These strong, stylized items fit well in a minimalist space with white walls.

One thing I should emphasize is that you must like the items you collect. As with any investment, you must be prepared to hold on to the items for a while before you decide to sell and hopefully reap a profit. Not all of my tips will turn out to be sure-fire winners, but I think that the list that follows contains a fair few items that will definitely show a profit if you hold on to them for long enough.

A

Anything with a clockwork movement that dates from the 1930s–70s is worth collecting, as these items tend to grow in value every year. Check the condition of anything you intend to buy, however, making sure that it is in full working order, as restoration can be expensive. Items in this category are often toys. Kept safely and bought together with their original boxes, they will show you a return on your money. In particular, look out for the mechanical toys that were given away with McDonalds Happy Meals, as these are proving collectable.

B

Barometers, particularly stick barometers from the 18th century and banjo barometers from the 19th century, are good investments. In particular, items bearing the mark of a London barometer-maker command a premium, and have shown a steady increase in value over the years.

C

Chinoiserie is a term used for Oriental-style decoration. Normally it depicts a landscape scene with figures and buildings, generally on a black or green background. My top tip here would be to try and collect some of the furniture which was retailed in the 1920s by Harrods. Like many other stores, Harrods was inspired by the Orient and decided to put out a range of Chinoiserie furniture. The bedroom suites look stunning, as do the sofas, chairs and side tables. Keep your eyes open for the Harrods mark and you will know that it is a top-quality piece. It won't come cheap, but it will hold its price.

D

Design from the 1960s, 1970s, and even the 1980s is increasingly valuable, with 20th-century furniture especially popular, as mentioned previously. However, there are a couple of things that you need to consider before you invest. Some of the top designers are being reproduced, so watch out for older designs that are still being made under licence. You do not have to spend a fortune on this modern furniture. Furthermore, there are many books published on this period, and you will have no trouble researching your item to find out what you are investing in. Over the next few years, I can assure you that you will see the prices rocket!

E

Early-18th-century porcelain is a good area in which to invest, as prices have tumbled recently, so they are bound to go back up. Eighteenth-century cups and saucers, which at one time were making £400–£500, can now be bought for as little as £150. This is the trend for most 18th-century porcelain at the moment. Look out for makers such as Chelsea, Bow, Lowestoft and Worcester, as these marks represent a blue chip investment and will surely increase in value when tastes change.

F

Fads and fashions came and went with great frequency during the 1970s, 1980s and 1990s. Those that came as quickly as they went are the ones you should be looking out for. Within a few years, they are sure to come into their own as part of the collectors' market. My main tip is to look for Japanese and Chinese imports of toy computers and hand-held games.

G

Glass comes in many shapes and forms; knowing what to invest in really comes down to your own personal taste. The big names in this field, such as Lalique, Baccarat and Daum, tend to represent blue chip investments. Some other stars to watch out for include Geoffrey Baxter, as the pieces he made at Whitefriars are making phenomenal amounts of money. In fact, Baxter's 'Bricklayer' vase is now worth £1,500–£2,000, whereas only six years ago you could have bought it for £100!

If you are on a budget, then glass paperweights from the 1970s are a good investment. Look for Perthshire and Kosta Boda, a Swedish glass company with some very distinctive designs. At the bottom end of the glass market look out for Venetian tourist glass, also known as Murano glass. Examples from the 1960s, which come in colourful shapes such as birds, fish and clowns, are relatively cheap at the moment, but prices are sure to rise soon.

H

Heroes are popular with collectors. If you want to make money in this area, you should think about the heroes of the future, not those of the past. When someone makes it to the top of their field, whether it is a pop star, sports star or movie star, there is normally something produced to commemorate their achievements. Try to invest in the limited-edition items rather than those that are mass-produced, as there is a wider market for such items.

I

Imari is one of Japan's most famous ceramic exports, although it was in fact Korean artisans who created the famous porcelain. First shipped from Japan to Holland in the 17th century, Imari ware was to influence many English potteries (including Masons, Royal Crown Derby and even Welsh Gaudy Ware) and is easily distinguished by its red, blue and white decoration. Expect to pay anywhere between £600–£800 for a good piece of 19th-century Imari; chargers are the most desirable pieces with collectors.

J

Jewellery can be a great investment, but please bear in mind that when you buy it from a retail unit, you will be paying up to 75 percent more than if it were for sale in an auction house.

Auction houses tend to price many items at scrap weight. Buying in a market like this can prove to be profitable, especially if the price of gold or silver rises rapidly. Many antiques magazines give a weekly update on the current price of gold and silver, so if you intend to invest in this area, keep your eyes open and sell at the right time. Hatton Garden, in London, is a great place to sell metals.

K

Childhood memories come flooding back whenever I see a **kaleido-scope**, as they provided a great form of entertainment in my youth. These gadgets date back to the late 19th century, when some excellent examples were made. Condition is really important, but presently they can be found relatively cheaply.

L

Lowestoft pottery is quite rare and difficult to find, but if you do come across it, it's a blue chip investment. The 18th-century factory produced porcelain that was very much in the style of Worcester, Bow and Chelsea.

M

Music boxes are charming items in which to invest. Many were made in Switzerland in the late 19th century; Nicole Ferris was a top producer and is a name to look out for. The value of a music box will be greater the more airs (tunes) it plays and the more decorative it is. Make sure that there are no teeth missing from the comb inside the box.

N

The **Nanking cargo** was carried on the *Geldermalsen*, a Dutch ship that sank in the South China Sea in 1752 and was salvaged in 1985. The cargo contained superb examples of 18th-century oriental porcelain, and many pieces can still be bought for about £50. Building a collection of items from a shipwreck is both interesting and enormous fun.

O

Oiliana is used to describe anything connected with the oil business, from oil and petrol cans to advertising signs and colanders. Most of these items date from the beginning of the 20th century, and oil cans bearing the names Shell, Castrol, Mobiloil or BP are most popular, especially those that once contained high performance oils. One of the lesser known companies to look out for is Pratts. Always check for condition and look out for unusual shapes.

Q

Making **quilts** was very popular in the homesteads of America. Most were made from scraps of old clothes or material, and would be stiffened with a piece of back paper, often old letters or pages from books; this evidence can help to give a date. The most desirable are those made in the American Colonial era of the early 19th century.

R

Restored items are only really acceptable if the item you are buying is exceptional or very rare. Otherwise I would recommend that you steer clear of anything that has been restored.

S

Stereoscope viewers were a Victorian invention. Cards were inserted into the viewer and a three-dimensional image appeared. Subject matter included animals, buildings, sightseeing attractions and even comics. You can expect to pay as little as £1 per card to as much as £30 for a rare example (eg. one from the First World War).

T

When investing in **technology,** do your homework first: read the relevant reference books and find out which models are the best items to collect. My personal tip would be to look for **televisions** from the 1950s and 1960s.

U

Film posters have had a popular following for many years, and **Universal Studios,** one of the biggest Hollywood studios, produced some of the best posters. Although the older posters will set you back a few hundred pounds, it is worth looking for posters for modern films, so ask your local cinema manager if you can have its posters once the theatre is finished with them.

V

Victor Vasarely was a Hungarian artist and architect who died in 1997. He is now considered by many to be the leading artist of the Op-Art movement. Although not everyone's cup of tea, his silk-screen prints are stunning, with a vibrant use of colour.

W

Walking sticks are enjoyable items to collect, with many different variations dating back to the Victorian and Edwardian periods, when a stick or a cane was an essential fashion accessory. Look out for examples with unusually shaped handles. It is worth bearing in mind that after the First World War there was a decline in walking-stick manufacture; even so, earlier sticks are the ones to collect.

Y

The light-brown or red grain of **yew wood** was much favoured by cabinet-makers in the 18th and 19th centuries, and mainly used as a veneer. In the late 20th century it was mass-produced for reproduction-style furniture, including military chests, Wellingtons, dining tables and chairs. These items will age favourably and can be obtained quite cheaply compared to early examples. Like rosewood and walnut, yew wood furniture will always command a premium.

Zeal: Beware of 'Auction Fever'!

I would like to use this chapter to refresh you about a couple of the most important things that you need to know about antiques and the auction business. I hope that by this point you have acquired a lot more knowledge of auctions and auction rooms than you had before you started to read this book. Remembering the advice and the important tips that are laid out for you in these pages could provide the edge you need to save you money when entering an auction room.

One of the most important things to avoid is zeal – that extreme feeling of fervour that you can experience when you are bidding on an item you feel you *must* have – in other words, 'auction fever'. Time and time again, when I have been on the rostrum I have witnessed auction fever take over bidders, making them lose all common sense.

To avoid this pitfall, you need to have a checklist at hand. By the time you come to bid, you will have seen the lots you want to buy at the preview day, had a good look around the saleroom, selected the goods you want to bid on and written down the price you are willing to pay for them.

Say, for example, that when the first lot comes under the hammer, you have secured it for £70, £30 less than your initial limit of £100. The question that you need to ask yourself when your next lot comes up for bid is whether you have saved or made £30. Now the next lot you wish to bid upon comes up – it is an oil painting, and you have set a limit of £200 for it. The tension in the saleroom is electrifying, you feel your heart quickening and you become oblivious to everything around you but the auctioneer. The sale opens at £100, and you are tempted to bid, but you have learnt the lessons demonstrated in this book and you wait for the bidding to slow down. It reaches £160 and the hammer almost falls – the time has come for you to bid. Everything is proceeding in textbook fashion, and you know you are doing everything correctly. Suddenly, the bidding rises to £190, and then to your limit of £200. Should you go to £210? Your mind races back to the previous lot you bought, where you saved that £30. Instinct tells you to put your hand up for one more bid. You bid, but immediately there is another bid for £220, and before you can put your hand down it is with you at £230. The next bid is £240, and you are above your limit once again. At this point, you need to watch yourself, as this is when your zeal for that item can take over, and auction fever can strike. You'll forget everything you've learned in this book, and will become overcome by passion. If you think this feeling is kicking in, then you must not raise your hand to bid.

As I have said many times, another lot will come along and it will be in your price bracket. You must never let emotions get the better of your finances. Keep your hand down and overcome the fever. I hope this is advice that will stand you in good stead throughout all the auctions you attend. It is very important and will save you a great deal of money.

Zoom in

Another piece of advice that you need to remember is to zoom in and inspect any items you want to bid on. For example, say you spot a wonderful piece of Sèvres china sitting in the viewing cabinet that would look beautiful on your Victorian chiffonier at home. It carries an estimate of £200–£400 in the catalogue. Although it is not marked as such, has it nonetheless been restored? Is it damaged at all? And is it really Sèvres, or is it a knock-off? Remembering everything you've learned in this book, you hold the piece up to a strong light to look for evidence of restoration, you flick the side of the dish to make sure it has got that nice ring to it (and not the dull thud that would suggest a hairline crack), and you check for the important Sèvres mark, so you know its advertised provenance is correct.

Now is the time for you to zoom in and inspect the piece even more closely. Ask yourself the following questions: How well is it painted? Is the gilding intact? Is it worn in certain places? If it is a painted landscape

133

Z IS FOR ZSOLNAY PÉCS

Zsolnay Pécs is a Hungarian ceramics company that I feel is grossly underrated. It was founded in Pécs by Miklos Zsolnay in 1853, and began by producing small stoneware and earthenware objects before gradually branching out into pottery, architectural ceramics (including tiles) and industrial goods. The factory was well-known for its technical skills, inventing a material called pyrogranite, which was used for architectural façades and was able to withstand frost and pollution. By the 1870s, the company's artistic division began to make decorative objects that blended historical motifs with those from nature.

Affected by international trends, Zsolnay decided to dispense with their more naive designs towards the end of the 19th century, moving in to the realms of Art Nouveau. By 1897 they had achieved international acclaim. Many vases made during that period incorporated an hourglass curve that was suggestive of the female form. These designs are highly prized among collectors, as are vases with an iridescent red glaze. This technique was developed by a chemist called Binsce Wartha, along with the gold lustre for which the factory is also renowned.

The company's initial success was, however, short-lived. With the Austro-Hungarian Empire in ruins after the First World War, the factory lost access to many of the materials it needed. It was not until the 1950s that Zsolnay started to regain some of its artistic creativity. Highlights since have included work by Victor Vasarely, who made a sculpture for the company in 1974. Thankfully, many fine examples of Zsolnay tiles and architectural designs from those early years survived the Second World War in Budapest and other Hungarian cities.

Largely state-owned, the factory still operates today and has an established ceramics studio that produces limited-edition objects and architectural pottery for contemporary buildings.

Z IS FOR ZEPPELIN

The Zeppelin was invented by Count Von Zeppelin at the turn of the last century and although the term has been used for other items, it strictly applies only to German airships of the First World War period. Memorabilia from Zeppelins, such as book-ends and desk stands, is fairly rare, but does turn up from time to time. Normally these objects will have been made from Zeppelin timber after an airship crashed or was crippled. Occasionally you will also find sketches, paintings and, more rarely, photographs of Zeppelins. German tin-plate toy Zeppelins dating from 1930 are also known to exist. An example in good condition can command over £1,000, so they are worth looking out for.

scene, how good is the perspective? Is it by one of the top Sèvres artists or one of the lesser painters? Remember, auction rooms do not mind how much time you spend viewing an item, and are more than happy to assist you with any questions you may have.

When zooming in to inspect lots, it is always worth taking along a strong magnifying glass or spyglass that will magnify the items. A spyglass can be very useful when you are reviewing a hand-painted piece of china, and a magnifying glass will come in handy when you want to look at a painting.

If you had seen the Sèvres piece at an antiques fair, it would be very important that you check its condition and ascertain whether or not it has been restored, as there is obviously less chance of being able to return the item (unless of course you know the dealer and have done business with him or her previously). Furthermore, it can be hard to zoom in on an item at a fair, as many stalls do not have bright lights; the chances are that you will not be able to check the porcelain to see if it has had any restoration done. You could thus take a small torch with you, or a halogen lamp, which would help you to spot restoration.

Auction Room Anecdotes

The life and times of an auctioneer are quite varied and, like a doctor, one is often on call 24 hours a day. After over 20 years in the auction business, during which time I sold almost £15 million-worth of antiques, I have come across many vendors, all of whom have same target in mind: to sell something that they think might have some value as an antique. The stories that follow are replete with lessons for aspiring antiques collectors, buyers and sellers; one is always wise to learn from the good decisions – and foibles – of others.

A Wish Comes True

In the late 1980s I received a call from a couple that lived on the out-skirts of Dover. On arriving at the house, which looked to me as if it had been furnished with bingo prizes, the sixth sense that auctioneers gain over the years (otherwise known as the 'X' Factor; see pages 122–125) kicked in – the feeling that there was something good in this house. I sat down and had a cup of tea with the couple, and discovered the reason for my call that day.

At the time, many houses were being repossessed as a result of rising interest rates and mortgage arrears, and it transpired that their daughter and her husband were among the many on the verge of losing their home; the couple wanted to sell some items in order to raise the necessary funds for their daughter. After a lengthy chat, I decided to have a look around their house. The couple pointed out a few items that they thought were possibly worth some cash, but regrettably many of these were worth pennies, not pounds. I had to point out to them that the reproduction items they owned would not go up in price, and the fact that they had only paid £10 for many of them did not make them an investment. I did, however, notice an old record player worth £50, a small Pembroke table worth about £80 and a nice mantle clock worth about £50. This was nowhere near the £2,000 they needed to raise in order to help their daughter.

As I walked into the main lounge, the hairs on my arms began to

PLATE 25

PLATE 26

PLATE 25: *These old advertising tins are now prized collector's items.*

OPPOSITE: *If you're not sure about an item, take a few notes and do some research at home before buying.*

ABOVE: *A helpful porter or auctioneer will point you in the right direction if you can't find the lot you're looking for.*

RIGHT: *Make sure the lot number corresponds with the description in the catalogue.*

OVERLEAF: *Try not to leave the saleroom empty-handed, but never dwell on the lot 'that got away' – there will always be another chance.*

PLATE 27

PLATE 28

PLATE 29

PLATE 30

PLATE 29: *Pop and rock memorabilia is now very collectable and so it is always worth rummaging through piles of old LPs to find that elusive rare example.*

OPPOSITE: *You can expect a jumbled mess in some general sales, but don't shirk from investigating thoroughly. You never know what might be lurking!*

ABOVE: *Make sure it's always clear what you are selling!*

RIGHT: *Jewellery can be a good investment, but tastes and values change constantly.*

PLATE 31

ABOVE: This original horn gramophone would be a great buy, but beware: there are fakes lurking out there. LEFT: The style and line of this Art Deco radio make it very collectable and worth much more than a more run-of-the-mill shape.

PLATE 32

stand on end. The sixth sense was kicking in and I just knew that there was something of value in the room. After a quick scan around, I noticed a particularly nice painted plate, which I recognized as being by Charlie Baldwin, a fine Royal Worcester artist. It was 16 inches in diameter and decorated with a flock of swans flying across a light blue background. I immediately pointed this out, but the clients quickly informed me that a friend knew all about this plate and wanted to buy it for their collection. They told me that it was an oriental plate made by Noritaki and was worth about £100. I couldn't contain my excitement any longer and asked if we could take it down and have a closer look, I turned it over and pointed out the mark on the back. The clients insisted that it was Noritaki and that they were going to sell it for £100. It took me a while to convince them that it was actually Royal Worcester. It was not until I pointed out that it was possibly worth £1,000–£1,500 that they changed their minds. At last, they were in a position to help their daughter.

Three weeks later, the plate was entered into the auction sale and was properly catalogued as a hand-painted Charles Baldwin charger produced by Royal Worcester, and depicting a flock of swans. The interest from both phone bidders, commission bids and bidders in the saleroom was phenomenal. The time was fast approaching for the plate to come under my ivory gavel. Out of the corner of my eye, I could see the client standing at the back of the saleroom. The bidding opened at £800 and soon flew to £1,500, with one remaining phone bidder and one left in the saleroom, it was going up in hundreds: £1,600, £1,700, £1,800, £1,900, £2,000. At £2,000 the bidder in the saleroom dropped out and the remaining bidder was on the phone at £2,000. Then, just as I was about to drop the hammer, another person in the saleroom raised their hand. The price went up from £2,200 to £2,400 to £2,600 and £2,800. The bidder in the saleroom dropped out. As I searched the room for another bid, I looked over to the clients and saw the excitement on their faces. The hammer dropped at the incredible price of £2,800. A few days later, the clients called me to tell me that they had secured their daughter's house. Their wish had come true.

An Elderly Client

Anyone who watched my primetime BBC television programme *Auction Man* will remember the many delightful characters that I encountered. Filming the show was quite a bizarre experience, as for six months I had a team of cameras and a sound crew following my every move. One day

I received a call from a charming elderly man who lived in assisted housing in Kent, and wanted me to value some items on his behalf. I went along, and the television crew came along too.

We entered a very small one-bedroom apartment and it was immediately obvious that there was nothing of any great value there. We sat down, had a cup of tea and the cameras started rolling. Although the show only included five minutes of my time with this client, I was actually with him for five hours. During this time, he explained to me that his main goal in his life was to raise money for a small charity, and so he wanted me to help him find some items to sell for this purpose.

During our lengthy chat, this elderly gentleman poured his heart out to me. He had lost his wife two years earlier and had never slept in the bed that he had shared with her since. He told me about his days in the war, his secret missions, his battles, his many awards and medals and the treasures that he had kept throughout his 80-odd years. I spent much of my time trying to convince him not to sell his many personal treasures, including his war medals, which were so obviously close to his heart.

One thing that never ceased to amaze me as an auctioneer was how many people were willing to sell personal items and things that were a part of their family history. Although I was in the business to make a profit, I always found it difficult to put such items into an auction. There were many times when I went to house clearances where the relatives of the deceased instructed me to clear the complete contents, including family photographs, diaries and treasured family pieces.

After persuading my elderly client to hold on to his more treasured items, I took a few pieces to sell on his behalf. These objects included a pair of damaged vases and some general nick-nacks. We sold the items and he raised under £100. Being the gentleman that he was, he donated it all to his charity. I have very fond memories of that special person, and after the show was aired, I received many letters to the effect that I had done the right thing to persuade the client to keep his family treasures. Several other war veterans also tried to contact him as a result of the programme.

The Caravan Party

Not all the stories that came out of the filming of *Auction Man* were melancholy. One particular incident, which still makes me chuckle when I think about it, was a day when I was called to a caravan park in Kent. When I was an auctioneer, I travelled about 50,000 miles a year looking for antiques and collectables to fill my auction room, and I answered every call, whether it was to a caravan park or a ten-roomed mansion. On this occasion, I drove 35 miles to meet the client, who lived in a smart caravan situated in a caravan park. When I arrived, the door was opened by an elderly man with the words: 'ere Doll, guess who's here, that Auction Man off the telly.' As I walked in, I suddenly realized what was going on – seated inside the caravan were half a dozen elderly people, each holding a tea cup and saucer and with a birthday cake on the centre table. As I walked in, they burst into a lively rendition of 'Happy Birthday' for the aforementioned Doll. I could not contain myself and started laughing, wondering what an earth I had walked into. It was then that the husband said, 'My wife loves you on the television and as a birthday present we thought we'd get you here to do some valuations for her on her birthday.'

Two hours later, after the birthday tea was finished, I asked what they wanted me to value. They replied that it was the teacups and saucers they were drinking from. I sat down, had another cup of tea, signed six autographs and valued their tea cups at £5–£10 each. It was not the most profitable of calls, but it was one of the most entertaining.

A Valuable Vase

I believe that auctions and auction rooms should be fun. On April 1st, 1988, I decided it would be a good April Fool's trick to fool my customers during a sale. At this point, my sales premises were in Folkestone. The building was approached by a steep flight of steps and was formerly an old railway church. It was an unmistakable building, full of character, with Gothic windows throughout. On sale days it could contain 60–100 people, both seated and standing. To the front of the saleroom was the rostrum, and being in this position was like over-looking a flock of sheep. Knowing where to get the bids and who to get the bids from is the hardest part of being an auctioneer in a very small saleroom. The night before this particular April auction, I was talking with my porter, and I told him the plan I had for sale day: to 'sell' a very small piece of Wedgwood jasperware with a normal value of £5–£6 for anywhere between £1,000-1,500. For the plan to work, I needed to place a couple of bidders in the saleroom. But there would be a final twist in the tale.

The auction day arrived, the saleroom was packed and the bidding was going well. It was a lively crowd. In those days, my porters used to hold up the items we were selling to show the prospective buyers. When it came to the Wedgwood item, one porter picked the small piece up out of the cabinet and held it up for everyone to see. I opened the bidding at £10 and it quickly flew up to £500. Ninety-nine percent of the people in the saleroom knew it was really only worth £10, and were puzzled as to why it was making so much money. I then announced that the piece was unique. My two fake bidders did not stop bidding, and the final hammer price was £1,000. As I dropped the hammer, the porter dropped the vase. The whole auction room gasped and the fake buyer stood up and demanded a full explanation. I took great delight as I watched the discussion between the two, while the rest of the auction room remained in shock! The porter said he had a lot to drink the night before and he was still shaking, which is why he had dropped the vase. As the auction room burst into laughter, the 'buyer' got up from his chair and stormed out of the saleroom. The following day I got a phone call from *The Sun* newspaper, which went on to put a small article in their paper about my April Fool's Day trick.

The Sleeper

Over the years I have had a few sleepers in my saleroom. As I mentioned earlier, a sleeper is an item entered into an auction sale and catalogued by the auctioneers to the best of their knowledge, but which actually has a much higher value. This particular sleeper was brought into my saleroom on a valuation day: a couple come in and and showed me an interestingly carved walking stick. I immediately recognized the intricate work involved in the piece and asked the clients what they knew about it. All they knew was that it had been passed through their family over the years, and that it had been stuck in their loft for the past three decades. Upon closer inspection of the walking stick, which was 3-feet tall, I started to think that it was quite a special item. Carved to the very top of the stick was the figurehead of a man; directly below that was a lady, and then two children, followed by a selection of other carved figures, including a baker, farmer and blacksmith. Although the carvings were quite crude, they were very detailed and dated to 1852. The stick also had some initials on it that could have indicated the name of a former owner or maker.

I informed the clients that I thought the walking stick could be an item of Welsh Folk Art, and that if the right collectors picked up on it, it could make between £400–£600. The couple were extremely happy with this valuation, as they had intended on giving the stick to a charity shop if it was worth below £100. As with all unusual collector's items, this particular lot created a large amount of interest, with emails and condition reports flying backwards and forward from the office computer. By the end of the viewing period we had six telephone lines booked for bidders, although no commission bids had been left, so I still really had no idea how much the item was actually going to sell for.

Unbeknown to me, one of the porters taking a phone bid had been instructed by the prospective buyer to carry on bidding. As I opened the bidding at £500, every phone line wanted to bid. It was only possible to take two bids at any one time, and the first two phone lines battled it out, sending the bidding up to £1,200. The first phone bidder dropped out, and the walking stick reached £1,500 before the second phone bidder dropped out. Eventually it was down to two bidders, as all of the other bidders had dropped out, one by one. The bidding was now at £2,200. The battle continued and finally reached £2,800. As the hammer dropped, there was a small round of applause from the auction crowd.

By now you may be asking the same question as I was. Why was this walking stick so valuable? I asked the buyer why he had paid such a lot for the piece. Looking through my reference books, it seemed that this sort of walking stick should only make between £500–£800 maximum. It was with great delight that he informed me that the walking stick was actually American Colonial Art and dated to 1853 – an extremely rare piece. A happy day was had by all – buyer, seller and auctioneer!

Night Of The Wolf

As an auctioneer, not all my calls were easy. There is one day I remember especially well. A regular customer and his wife asked if I would do a valuation on his father's estate. I was more than happy to do this, so they gave me the address and I realized it was quite far out in the country (not that this was a problem, as I often travelled miles on my quest for antiques).

I drove up a dark country lane and approached a large Georgian house that was set in its own grounds. I soon realized that I was the first to arrive, so while waiting for the clients I got out of the car. I immediately heard the sound of loud barking, which persuaded me to get back into the car. Five or so minutes later my clients turned up. I got out of the car to greet them and turned to see an enormous Alsatian dog barking viciously at the gate. The client asked if I was scared of dogs, and I replied that I was not, as I have a chihuahua and a Yorkshire terrier. He insisted that this Alsatian, which was a guard dog, was quite tame. While he was telling me this, he opened the front gate, and, before I knew it, the dog jumped up at me and tried to bite my face. I managed to elbow the dog off me, but it bit my hand and proceeded to bite my leg and maul my back. The client eventually pulled the dog off me and bundled it in to the outhouse, commenting that it may be hungry. Hungry? It had just taken lumps out of me and eaten half my suit!

I continued into the house, where I began to value its contents; this took about an hour. The client was obviously concerned about my well-being and kept asking if I was OK. The back of my leg was bleeding and my suit was torn. When I had finished my valuation, I got into my car and the shock of the canine attack hit me – I almost passed out. As I was driving home, I wondered why the dog had gone for me.

While we were discussing the incident over dinner, my wife reminded me that the day before I had been wearing a wolf-skin fur coat. I had bought the coat to keep me warm while I filmed a television pro-gramme for the BBC in Newark (if you have ever been to Newark antiques fair on a cold and windy day you will know why I needed it!).

In retrospect, I am sure that the dog attacked me because he thought I was a rogue wolf! Nowadays, whenever I visit a house with an Alsatian dog, I ask its owner to lock it up in the kitchen!

From Bargain Hunt to Auction Man

Back in 2000 I was approached by the BBC to host four shows for the increasingly popular daytime show called *Bargain Hunt*, presented by David Dickinson. It was a popular format whereby two teams of con-testants were given £200 to spend at an antiques fair and then sell on at an auction sale. Little did I know the effect the show would have on my life. On the day they were due to film with us, a team of cameras, sound engineers, researchers, directors and producers all turned up in the sale-room. I was introduced to Mr Dickinson and we had a good old chin wag, spending most of the next two hours discussing furniture, bronzes, paintings and the antiques trade. I found David one of the most knowl-edgeable people in the antiques trade that I had met for a long time.

After I was wired up for sound it was time for David and I to do our 'auctioneer's chat' about the items bought by the teams. To the shock and horror of the directors I told them that one of the items, a chair which was riddled with woodworm and had been bought for £50, should be thrown on the skip. The team's other item was a table, for which they had paid £100 but which was clearly a marriage. I told them the best thing they could do was to burn it! Lo and behold, the director liked this honest approach, especially as they had not had this sort of brutal remark from an auctioneer on the show before. What I had said proved to be a reality in the sale proper, as most of the items I had condemned actually lost money, but that is quite the norm in *Bargain Hunt*!

A couple of days after the team had left I received a call from the producers asking if I would like to go to Paris to film two shows there. On this occasion I was to be an expert and advise the teams on what to buy. It was a great experience, if not rather daunting, but I then went on to film a further 35 daytime shows, all with David Dickinson. Over a period of time we became good friends and most of our conversations are normally about antiques.

Whilst I was filming for *Bargain Hunt* I was approached by the BBC and asked if I would like to do a documentary about my life as an auctioneer and the running of my auction house in a new show. This was to be shown on prime-time television, and after six months' filming my show *Auction Man* was aired on BBC1 on a Wednesday evening. From being an antiques expert on *Bargain Hunt* I then became known as the Auction Man. The show was a great success and led to other television work, including over 30 shows for Terry & Gabby on Channel 5, appearances on *Crimewatch* as an antiques expert and on *Ready, Steady, Cook* with the new presenter of *Bargain Hunt*, Tim Wonnacott.

For various reasons in 2004 I decided it was time to sell my auction business and move on. After I had exchanged contracts on the auction room I was approached by Channel 4 and ask to present a television show called *Name Your Price*. Once again, this was an antiques show based in auction rooms – my home territory. With 30 shows completed, it was aired in 2005. The show had a simple format whereby we offered three opinions on what we thought a specific item would sell for at auction. The viewer then had a chance to guess which expert was right for the chance to win £500. Just in case you were wondering, I didn't always get it right!

Finally, I hope you have enjoyed this book and that it helps you on the path to enjoyment and financial success in the fabulous world of antiques and auctions.

Glossaries

AUCTION ROOM GLOSSARY

Absentee bid: Leaving a bid with the auction house so that it can bid on your behalf.

Auction fever: The situation that occurs when a bidder forgets the true value of a lot and bids like a headless chicken.

Auction preview: The days that are allocated for prospective buyers to view all of the items and lots in the saleroom.

Auctioneer: The person sitting on the rostrum wielding the gavel and monitoring the bids.

Bidders: The people in the saleroom who are attempting to buy goods.

Bidding off the wall: A term used for an auctioneer who is taking bids from the wall to get up to a reserve price.

Buyer's premium: The sum that is added to the hammer price and paid to the auction house. It ranges from 5–25 percent of the final bid, and then VAT is usually added.

Cashier: The person who has the pleasure of taking your money when you have bid successfully on a lot.

Catalogue: The publication available from the auctioneer on viewing days and sale days. It contains a complete list of all items entered into the auction.

Commission bid: A bid that is written on a form supplied by the auction house so that they can execute the bid for you.

Condition report: A detailed description of the state of a lot. It can be obtained from the auctioneers via email, phone, post or in person.

Dealers: These are the professionals – dealers in antiques – whom you often see huddled together in an auction room.

Defaulting on a bid: When you do not fulfil a bid. This situation can prove very costly, as the auction house can pursue a claim against you if you do not pay for and collect the lot you bid upon in the auction.

Estimates: These figures are provided as a guide to prospective buyers, and are normally based around a reserve price (see opposite).

Hammer price: The final price you pay when the auctioneer's hammer drops.

Invoice: This will list each lot you have purchased, how much you paid for each lot and the total amount you have spent, with the buyer's premium and VAT added.

Lot number: The number given to each item coming up for auction.

Paddle number: The specific number that is allocated to each buyer after registration (see below).

Porters: These are the happy faces that walk around the saleroom and normally point out the lots as they are coming under the hammer. They will also help you pack and move your goods at the end of the sale.

Registering to bid: This is normally done in the head cashier's office. You are required to register with your name, address and some form of identification. Once this is completed, you will be given a paddle number with which to bid in the auction.

Reserve price: The reserve price is the lowest price at which a seller is willing to sell their item. The reserve price is never disclosed to bidders. A seller might specify a reserve price if he or she is unsure of the real value of his or her item and would like to reserve the right to refuse to sell the item if the market value is below a certain price. This price is agreed between the auction room and the vendor.

Selling rate: The number of lots the auctioneer normally sells per hour. This is usually between 80 and 300.

Storage charges: The charge you have to pay if you are late in clearing your items from the saleroom.

Telephone bid: A pre-arranged phone link that is booked with the auctioneer for the lots that you would like to bid on. This method allows bidders to remain anonymous.

Terms of business: The legal jargon that is normally displayed at the back of the saleroom or in the catalogue. This usually includes buyers' and vendors' rights and obligations, conditions of purchase and sale, commission payments and much more – always read these before doing business at any auction house.

Terms of payment: Most auction houses accept cheques, cash and all major credit cards.

Valuations: The price given to an item by the head valuer of the saleroom.

Vendor: A technical term for the seller of goods at auction houses.

Withdrawn lots: Items taken out of the sale by the auction house.

BAROMETER GLOSSARY

Aneroid barometer: This type of barometer uses a sealed, evacuated chamber instead of mercury to measure air pressure. It was invented in the mid-19th century.

Banjo barometer: A type of wheel barometer, so named because of its resemblance to a banjo.

Barograph: An aneroid barometer with a self-recording mechanism that is activated by clockwork.

Hygrometer: An instrument that measures humidity.

Stick barometer: A barometer housed in a slimline case.

Wheel barometer: A barometer with a round register plate, so called because of its shape.

CLOCK GLOSSARY

Automation: Figures that move or strike on the hour and the quarter-hour.

Balance wheel: The mechanism that controls the movement of a watch or a clock.

Bezel: The ring that secures the glass cover to the dial on a watch or a clock.

Calendar aperture: The small window on some dials that displays the day of the month and sometimes the month itself.

Chapter ring: The part of the dial on which the hour numbers are painted, engraved or attached.

Escapement: The part of the clock that regulates it and provides the impulse to the chain, pendulum or balance.

Hood: The part of a longcase clock that lifts off the top to provide access to the movement.

Pendulum: The device that swings at a fixed rate and controls the timekeeping.

Repeat button: A small device that lets the clock repeat the last hour or quarter-hour when a cord is pulled or a button is pressed.

FURNITURE GLOSSARY

Apron: The decorative, shaped skirt of wood that runs under the drawers and between the legs of a table or feet of a chest.

Ballester: The shaped turning or slender pillar with a bullbats base that is used on the legs and pedestals of tables.

146

Banding: Decorative veneers used around the edges of tables, drawers and other items of furniture.

Barley twist: A spiral shape normally favoured for turned legs during the second half of the 19th century. The pattern is still in use today.

Bergère: A French term that is applied to chairs with caned backs and seats.

Boulle work: A form of marquetry using brass and tortoiseshell that proved very popular in the 19th century.

Bow front: An outwardly curved front that is found mainly on chests of drawers or on sideboards.

Break front: A term normally used for a piece of furniture with a protruding centre section.

Brush-in slide: The pull-out slide found on the top of a chest of drawers, normally associated with 18th-century bachelor's chests.

Bun foot: A flattened version of a ball foot that was very popular in Victorian times.

Bureau: A writing desk with a tall front that normally encloses a fitted interior; many also have drawers below.

Cabriole leg: A curving S-shaped leg used on tables and chairs; synonymous with the 18th century.

Canterbury: A small container used to hold sheet music or papers.

Chesterfield: Normally a deep-buttoned upholstered settee with no wood showing.

Cheval mirror: A tall, freestanding dressing mirror that is supported by two uprights.

Chinoiserie: Oriental-style decoration or a lacquered pattern applied to furniture.

Claw and ball foot: A support modelled as a ball gripped by a claw.

Commode: A highly decorated chest of drawers or cabinet that is also called 'bombe-shaped'.

Console table: A table that stands against a wall, normally between windows. These sometimes have matching mirrors, and can come in pairs.

Corner chair: A chair with backed splats on two sides that is intended to stand in the corner of the room.

Davenport: A small, compact writing unit that normally has a flight of drawers and a sloped top for writing.

Drop-in seat: An upholstered seat frame that sits in the main framework of a chair.

Drop leaf table: A table with a fixed central section and hinged sides.

Figuring: The natural grain of wood seen in veneer.

Finial: A decorative turned knob normally applied to the top of bookcases and bureaux.

Frieze: The framework immediately below a tabletop.

Harlequin: A term used to describe a set of chairs that are similar but do not match exactly.

Inlay: Normally brass, mother of pearl or veneer, these are set into the surface of a solid piece of furniture or wood.

Ladderback: A chair with a series of horizontal back rails.

Lion's paw feet: A foot carved as a lion's paw; this style was very popular in the 18th century, but is also found on brass castors from the early 19th century.

Loo table: A large table that is normally circular.

Marquetry: A highly decorative form of inlay using numerous veneers.

Ormolu: A mount or article that is gilded or gold coloured.

Over-mantel mirror: A mirror designed to hang over a mantelpiece.

Papier mâché: Pulped paper that is moulded to make small trays or small items of furniture.

Parquetry: A geometrical pattern made from small pieces of veneer.

Patina: The build up of wax and dirt that gives old furniture its unique look.

Pedestal desk: A popular flat desk, usually with a leather top, that stands on two flights of drawers.

Pembroke table: A small side table with two small flaps.

Pie-crust top: The carved or moulded decoration at the edge of a table.

Pole screen: An adjustable fire screen.

Runners: The strips of wood on which drawers slide in and out.

Side table: Any table designed to stand against the wall.

Sofa table: Normally a rectangular-shaped table with two small, hinged flaps at the ends, designed to stand directly behind a sofa.

Stretchers: The horizontal bars that strengthen chairs.

Stuff-over seat: A chair that is upholstered over the seat rails.

Teapoy: A small 19th-century piece of furniture designed for holding tea leaves.

Toilet mirror: A small dressing mirror with a drawer below.

Trefoil: Any item that resembles a clover leaf.

Wot-not: A stand with open shelves of the type popular in the 19th century.

Wheel-backed chair: A chair with a circular back and spoke-like support.

POTTERY AND PORCELAIN GLOSSARY

Applied decoration: Anything that is attached to a piece rather than being a part of the main body.

Baluster vase: A vase with a curved shape and a narrow stem or neck.

Basalt: A black volcanic stoneware, used frequently by Wedgwood.

Blue and white: A general term used for porcelain and earthenware that normally has a Chinese decoration.

Blanc de Chine: A very translucent type of Chinese porcelain that is still being produced today. It is left unpainted and has a thick glaze.

Bone china: A term used for English porcelain.

Cabinet ware: Plates, cups and saucers made for display rather than for everyday use. These pieces are normally hand-painted and of very good quality.

Cancellation mark: One or two strokes through the factory mark that let the buyer know that the item is flawed and not of the maker's normal standard.

Cartouche: A decorative oval frame that is set within the porcelain and normally hand-painted or printed.

Celadon: A term for the green glaze that is often used on Chinese stoneware.

Chocolate cup: A large cup with two handles, a cover and a matching saucer.

Coffee can: A straight-sided cylindrical cup with no handles; this style was made famous by Sèvres.

Commemorative ware: Any item that commemorates an event, such as a wedding, jubilee or a battle.

Cow creamer: A cream jug in the form of a cow. These items were very popular in the late 18th and 19th centuries.

Crackleware: A form of decoration used on an item, normally Chinese.

Crazing: Tiny surface cracks in the glaze of the porcelain that has been caused by technical defects.

Delft ware: Earthenware made in the Netherlands with a tin glaze (see below).

Enamels: The bright colours applied to pottery and porcelain as over-glazed decoration (see below).

Faïence ware: Tin-glazed earthenware that is normally made in France, Germany and other European countries.

Famille rose or verte: Chinese decoration of either pink (rose) or green (verte) enamel.

Firing crack: Damage to pottery that has occurred during firing.

Flambé: A bright crimson glaze.

Flat back: A term used for a Staffordshire figure that has a plain, flat back so that it stands easily on a mantlepiece or fireplace.

Gilding: A term used for the application of gold, normally to the banding of porcelain made in the Chinese manner.

Impressed mark: A mark that is indented into the piece by the factory makers.

Incised mark: A mark that is scratched into the surface.

Ironstone china: A type of English stoneware made famous by Masons.

Jardinière: A plant or flower container; these are sometimes formed of two pieces with a matching stand.

Lead-glazed: A type of transparent glaze that incorporated lead oxide.

Loving cup: A twin-handled cup that is normally urn-shaped. This style was made by many potteries.

Over-glazed: This is decoration painted or printed onto the piece of pottery or porcelain after glazing.

Parian ware: Unglazed biscuit porcelain similar to Parian marble. It was very popular in 19th-century England and the United States for figures and figurines.

Pearl ware: A very durable form of white porcelain that was particularly popular at Wedgwood.

Porcelain: A translucent white ceramic that is very fragile.

Pottery: A generic term for all ceramics, excluding porcelain.

Puzzle jug: An unusual jug with a globular body and three or seven spouts at the rim.

Rococo: A popular style of mid-18th century decoration, which is normally asymmetric with the use of scrolls.

Soft-paste porcelain: Another term for porcelain which is made in a particular way.

Staffordshire: A generic term for English pottery made in the Midlands.

Studio pottery: Pottery that has been individually designed and crafted.

Tea bowl: A small cup with no handle inspired by the Oriental fashion for tea. They were mass-produced.

Terracotta: Lightly fired red earthenware that is not usually glazed.

Tin glaze: An opaque white glaze containing tin, popular in the 18th and 19th centuries and often used on majolica and toby jugs.

Transfer print: A form of general decoration using a printed engraving.

SILVER GLOSSARY

Assay mark: A date-stamp given to silver produced in Britain, Ireland and Scotland that indicates it has been properly tested and is pure.

Beading: A decorative border of small beads around an item of silver.

Bezel: The inner rim of a cover, it is normally in descriptions of coffee pots and teapots.

Britannia standard: A rare mark used on British silver between 1690–1720, which indicates goods of a high quality.

British plate: An early version of silver-plating, which dates from the 1830s–1850s, and was thereafter called electroplating (see below).

Canteen: A box used to contain cutlery, it normally houses a full service for 8–12 people.

Cartouche: A decorative frame or panel that normally surrounds a coat of arms.

Castor: A two-piece item that is used for sprinkling salt, pepper or sugar.

Chalice: Another name for a goblet or wine cup of the type often used at Catholic or Church of England services.

Charger: A large dish or plate which is normally circular or oval in shape.

Chasing: Decoration that is worked into a silver item with a hammer or a punch. This sort of pattern is raised above the surface.

Cruet: The framework for castors and bottles containing condiments, such as salt, pepper, oil or vinegar.

Dish ring: An unusual item of silver normally used to keep hotplates away from the table surface. These pieces usually have concave sides, pierced work and animal shapes. They are similar to an item of silver called a potato ring and are almost exclusively Irish.

Electroplating: Also known as E.P.N.S or EP on copper, this is silver applied over a copper of nickel alloy, and is a style that was in use from about 1840.

Ewer: A large jug with a lip that is often part of a set with a basin. It is sometimes used to contain water so that diners can wash their hands during meals.

Filigree: Open decorative panels with small silver beads. Today's filigree normally comes from Spain, India or Africa.

Flatware: Technically this is a term for all flat objects such as plates and silver, although more recently it has been applied to services of spoons and forks.

Floating or erasure: To remove an existing coat of arms and replace it with another.

151

Gadrooning: A border around the edge of an item, usually formed from a succession of leaves and flutes.

Gilding: A method of applying a gold finish to silver or electroplated items.

Right cut: A common form of engraving that makes the designwork stand out more sharply.

Salver: A flat dish that is similar to a serving tray but has no handles.

Sheffield plate: A silver substitute that was used in the early 18th century. It was made by binding and fusing sterling silver and copper.

Sterling silver: An English term for silver that contains at least 9.25 percent pure silver.

Recommended Auction Houses

Listed below is a selection of auction houses which I think offer a good service. Website addresses and contact numbers are correct at the time of writing (January 2006). A quick search on the internet will help you identify many other alternative salerooms and sources of advice.

Cameo Auctions
Kennet Holme Farm
Bath Road
Midgham
BERKSHIRE
RG7 5UX
01189 713772
www.cameo-auctioneers.co.uk

Dreweatt Neate
Donnington Priory Salerooms
Donnington
Newbury
BERKSHIRE
RG14 2JE
01635 553553
www.dnfa.com/donnington

Dreweatt Neate
Tunbridge Wells Salerooms
The Auction Halls
Linden Park Road
The Pantiles
Tunbridge Wells
KENT
TN2 5QL
01892 544500
www.dnfa.com/tunbridgewells

David Lay
The Penzance Auction House
Alverton
Penzance
CORNWALL
TR18 4RE
01736 361414
www.invaluable.com/partnerpages

Horner's the Auctioneers
Old Norwich Road
Acle
NORFOLK
NR13 3BY
0800 975 4416 or 01493 750225
www.horners.co.uk

Philip Serrell
The Malvern Saleroom
Barnards Green Road
Malvern
WORCESTERSHIRE
WR14 3LW
01684 892314
www.serrell.com

Shapes Auctioneers & Valuers
Bankhead Avenue
Sighthill
EDINBURGH
EH11 4BY
0131 4533222
www.shapesauctioneers.co.uk

Sotheby's (London)
34–35 New Bond Street
LONDON
W1A 2AA
0207 293 5000
www.sothebys.com

Tennants
The Auction Centre
Leyburn
NORTH YORKSHIRE
DL8 5SG
01969 623780
www.tennants.co.uk

Rupert Toovey
Spring Gardens
Washington
WEST SUSSEX
RH20 3BS
01903 891955
www.rupert-toovey.co.uk

Further Reading

The books detailed below will help you learn more about particular aspects of collecting antiques. The list is by no means exhaustive, and there are many other interesting titles worth looking out for in bookshops or ordering through your local library. Remember that for price guides – such as *Miller's Antiques Price Guide* – you will need to consult the most up-to-date editions.

Art Price Annual published by artprice.com.

Books–Auction Record edited by Wendy Heath, published by Dawson UK (1999).

Encyclopaedia of British Pottery and Porcelain Marks by Geoffrey A.Godden, published by Hutchinson (1968).

The Charlton Standard Catalogue of Wade Whimsical Collectables by Pat Murray, published by Francis Joseph (1997).

Collecting Kitchenware by Christina Bishop, published by Miller's Publications (1995).

Decorative Arts, 1950s by Charlotte and Peter Fiell, published by Taschen (2000).

Design of the 20th Century by Charlotte and Peter Fiell, published by Taschen (2000).

English Goldsmiths and Their Marks by Charles James Jackson, published by Dover Publications (1965).

Erotic Antiques by Annette Curtis, published by Lyle Publications (1990).

Hislop's Art Sales Index edited by Duncan Hislop, published annually.

Miller's 20th-century Design Buyer's Guide by Paul Rennie, published by Mitchell Beazley (2003).

Miller's Collecting Furniture: The Facts at Your Fingertips by Christopher Payne, published by Mitchell Beazley (1998).

Moorcroft: A Guide to Moorcroft Pottery by Paul Atterbury and Beatrice Moorcroft, published by Richard Dennis (1993).

The National Trust Manual of Housekeeping published by Butterworth Heinemann (2005); the essential guide to the care of antiques and interiors in the home.

Oak Furniture: The British Tradition by Victor Chinnery, published by Antique Collectors Club (1999).

Poole Pottery edited by Lesley Hayward and Paul Atterbury, published by Richard Dennis (1999); this book contains a comprehensive catalogue of all Poole pottery works.

The Royal Doulton Collector's Handbook edited by Kevin Pearson and Francis Salmon (1986).

Royal Doulton Figures by Desmond Eyles, Richard Dennis, Louise Irvine and Valerie Baynton, published by Richard Dennis (1994 edition).

Sleepers: in Search of Lost Old Masters by Philip Mould, published by Fourth Estate (1995).

Staffordshire Portrait Figures by P.D.Gordon Pugh, published by Barrie & Jenkins (1981).

The Wade Collectors Handbook by Robert Prescott Walker, E.J.Folkard and F.J.Salmon, published by Francis Joseph (1997).

Index

Acknowledgements

Writing this book has been great fun! I would like to especially thank my lovely wife Lesley, who spent numerous cold hours in my office typing out my Dictaphone tapes. Thanks also to the Criterion Auction Rooms for letting me use their saleroom for some of the photographs in this book. Finally, a personal thanks to my very good mate David Dickinson for writing such an individual foreword.